The Life and Times
of an Ossick Lad

GEOFFREY ELLERAY

The Life and Times
of an Ossick Lad

An Autobiography

The Life and Times of an Ossick Lad
was first published in 2010 by
Geoffrey Elleray
in association with
Long House Publishing Services, Cumbria, UK

© Geoffrey Elleray, 2010

Production and design by Kate Kirkwood
Printed by Badger Press Ltd, Bowness on Windermere

ISBN 978-0-9556437-3-6 (pb)

Contents

List of Photographs
&
Appendices

24. Me in working boiler suit
25. Me with beard
26. Our wedding, 10 November 1962
27, 28. Outside Colton Church
29. Loading hay at the Snowie's farm
30. Snowie's caravan
31. Susan and David flying kites at the Snowie's farm
32. Presenting Alisa Hampshire with the ASNT Technician of the Year Award
33. Me and Gail from *Coronation Street*, at the Prince's Trust 25th Anniversary
34. Me and Doreen at the same event
35. Dad's 80th birthday
36. En route in Germany with Doreen and Mr and Mrs Bowyer
37. Bungalow, "Duneden", Dunnet Head, north of Scotland
38. At work, with an x-ray set, NDT department

Appendices

This book is dedicated

to my loving wife Doreen who has made such a large contribution to my life, providing me with everything that could have been expected and more;

to my children, Susan and David, and to all my grandchildren who have made my life complete;

to my sister Enid who was with me from the beginning;

to my father who was always telling me to get my hands out of my pockets and into somebody else's;

and to my mother who nurtured me in my early days.

Acknowledgements

I would like to thank the following for their involvement in helping me to bring the living experience to publication: Mrs Parke (Miss Turney) for her initial involvement when I was starting out on the book; Ray Wilson for his supporting knowledge, digital imaging work and general advice; Raymond Wilkinson for verification of the scouting information; Hilary Howker for information on Bank End; John Imlach and David Kaine for guidance on original drafts and the way ahead; Liz Nutall for pre-publication advice; Kate Kirkwood for editorial, proofreading, design and general publishing support; all others who have directly or indirectly encouraged me to take a more open view of the potential regarding the information presented.

Copyright

Preface

"Ossick" is the local name for two adjacent villages which nestle on the Furness Peninsula between the Furness fells and Morecambe Bay, approximately 3 miles south of Ulverston and 7 miles north of Barrow-in-Furness, in northwest England. Their place names are Great Urswick and Little Urswick but they are known locally as "Girt Ossick" and "Lile Ossick" (the "s" pronounced as an "s" not a "z"). I grew up and have spent many of my days in and around the "Ossick" area; it was the place that formed me and has been the backdrop to my life.

On my death there may be nobody who is totally familiar with my background; even my immediate family will not know the full recipe I was made from. Those near to me will be familiar with most of the ingredients but not know how they fit together to make the complete me. This book may provide answers to the questions: "who was he?" and "what did he do?" and I hope the recollections I have enjoyed gathering here will acknowledge the people who influenced me and explain the direction my life has taken.

I anticipate this book may be of interest to my family, relatives and friends, as well as to "Ossickownians", work associates, educationalists, career advisors, psychologists, social historians and, perhaps, avid biography readers.

The views and opinions expressed here are those of the author and are not intended to offend or be disrespectful to any person or organisation.

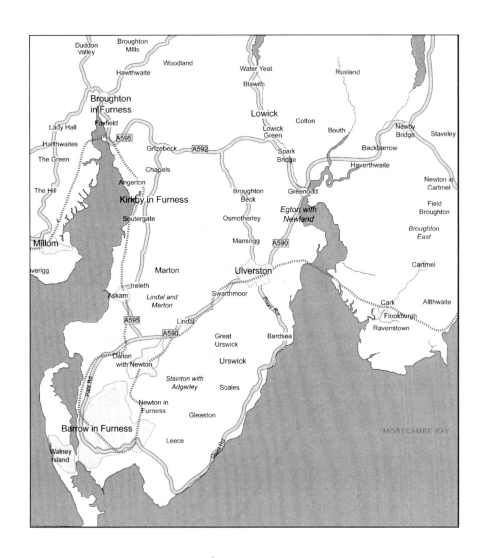

Map of Furness, South Cumbria

CHAPTER ONE

1938–1950
Aged 0–11 Years
Background, Early Days, Primary School

"Slightly tarnished but still valuable and legal tender"

Background

It was in Ulverston Cottage Hospital on the 13th December 1938 that I was born, and my birth was followed 15 minutes later by that of my sister. We were the twins of Ernest and Elsie Mary Elleray.

Being born six weeks premature we were both extremely under weight, weighing in at around 3lb 4 oz each, and were not expected to survive. I think I was slightly smaller than my sister although she may say it was the other way round. Later in life I found a handwritten note by my mother: "Geoffrey in hospital 1 month but for 3 days weighed 4lb. 4ozs and Enid in hospital 5 weeks but for 3 days weighed 4lb. 10 ozs". As there was a high risk of death we were named immediately, Geoffrey and Enid.

Having survived the drama of birth our family home was to be at No 1, Bank End Terrace, Great Urswick. The house was built from stone quarried from a small limestone quarry at Bank End by my grandfather on my mother's side, Robert Shuttleworth, and his two sons, William and Jimmy. The construction had taken place during 1933 and was not without its problems, suffering from flooding and walls collapsing due to frost and other factors. The finished house was passed over to my mother through a mortgage with Furness and South Cumberland Permanent Building Society. The house cost approximately £400. This was prior to her marriage to my father in January 1934 at Holy Trinity Church, Ulverston.

I lived with my parents in this family house until my marriage in November 1962. Later, my sister Enid moved out following her marriage to Alan in 1966. I moved to Ulverston whilst Enid moved three houses away to the other end of the semi-detached dormer bungalows, No 4, the one adjacent to Bank End. Enid and Alan still live in this house.

As records from July 1911 show, My grandfather owned the Bank End Estate, a smallholding encompassing five to six acres of adjacent land to the north and west, the areas numbered 438, 439, 443 and 444 on the map in Appendix A). He lived there with Cicely, my grandmother. As a builder and contractor he built two pairs of semi-detached bungalows to the north and alongside the road from Pennington to Urswick (area 439). This is known as Bank End Terrace. He also developed the rougher, craggy land to the back, where he built a further 3 pairs of semi-detached bungalows called Craglands Park. Prior to this he had already built a detached bungalow on the crag known as Heaning Wood which is virtually central to the estate. He built this with the intention of moving in with my grandmother but my grandmother wouldn't move from the Bank End house.

After the death of my grandfather (on 13th March 1937) and my grandmother (on 22nd November 1940) Bank End was passed on, in equal shares, to their children – two sons and two daughters, one of whom was my mother.

Bank End property consisted of two separate domestic attached houses which were let out to families who, because of the war, had to move from Barrow. Mr and Mrs Moralee, along with Mr Braithwaite, lived in my grandparent's house and Mrs Helm lived in the other. The farm buildings were let out to Reuben Stables, a farmer from the village. The other buildings were let to my father as a smallholding where he used the yard to park, repair and service his cattle truck. Another building on the property was a small garage which was rented to the local policeman, Bob May, for his small Austin Seven car. In May 1955 the Bank End property was sold to John Wood, a farmer from out of the village, for £1,750.

The Craglands properties to the north east had direct access from Bank End by a track known as The Bank. It also had a vehicle access from the road known as Stone Dike Lane. All these houses were within approximately 500 yards of the main farm buildings. The farm building and house were 50 yards from the Derby Arms public house and the same distance to Bankfield, a large Victorian house in its own grounds. This formed the basis of a close knit community.

No 1, Bank End Terrace would have then been classed as a 'modern' house as it had a kitchen, back kitchen – or scullery as it was known – pantry, sitting room, two bedrooms upstairs and a room downstairs which was used as my bedroom later in the adolescent stage, a bathroom and toilet. The bungalow, as it was called, was a dormer type and had stairs. On the north side was a glass-covered porch which had a coal bunker and access to a wash house with its cast iron solid fuel boiler. There was a garden to the front, facing east, and a side garden facing north, as well as a space at the rear which in the early days had a walk way direct to Bank End. This access pathway allowed my mother and her parents to go to and fro without going on the main road.

The kitchen was the everyday living area. We also had a back kitchen where all the meals were prepared, with a pantry leading off. It had a coal-fired black Chattenette range fireplace with a back boiler to heat the water, an oven for baking and a smaller oven above in which the kindling for the week was stored. It was my duty from a young age to provide the kindling. Most of the time there was plenty of old wood and boards about because my father was always replacing floor boards and gates in his cattle truck. But there was a time when good splitting wood was not available so I worked out how many pieces of wood it took to light a fire and I assessed this at seven; therefore as long as I produced 49 pieces for the week I thought I had fulfilled my duty, but I was called a miserable bugger and told my mother should not be reliant on this sort of rationing and I had to go hunting for additional supplies. The washing up was also carried out in the back kitchen in a deep rectangular sink which my father referred to as the slopstone. There was also an electric cooker and large table for baking. In the early fifties we had the luxury of one of the first domestic "Hoover" electric washing machines which had an attached folding ringer, and the lid of the tub also served as a tray to collect the clothes after wringing the excess water from them. The dirty water from the washer had to be drained by siphoning down an attached rubber hose.

The air in this kitchen was frequently full of a smoky blue haze, not just from the coal fire but from my father's habit of smoking both a pipe and cigarettes. The ritual included peeling off layers of black twist tobacco with his penknife for the pipe, supplemented by 40 full-strength Capstan cigarettes a day. This was accepted as part of the environment, although it may have affected my sister's health because she suffers severely from asthma and bronchial problems, but it appears not to have caused me any problems.

Another contributing factor to the air pollution may have been a valour paraffin stove that was used to temporarily heat the back kitchen, the porch and our bedroom in winter. When lit the stove produced a very regular circled pattern of light on the ceiling from the flame projection through the holes in its top. It is difficult to estimate how much fumes were given off. Every gallon of paraffin burnt produced approximately a pint of water so there could also have been an element of condensation.

My parents were in their late thirties when my sister and I were born, my father 38 years old and mother 36. My father was a motor mechanic and driver, predominantly occupied with moving livestock. He was a driver for Dick Christian from Ulverston, but the carrier licence permitted him to move anything and it was classed as a Livestock and Furniture Removal business. In 1942, a few years after my birth, my father had the opportunity to buy the business from Mr Christian for around £200 and he took a loan from a colleague to finance the deal. My mother was always a housewife and never went out to work.

We would perhaps not have been classed as poor but with being war babies money and circumstances were tight and uncertain. We were fortunate in that my father's work provided us with a fairly secure family situation, compared to other people in the village, some of whom were going through hard times.

My father was one of five children and my mother one of four so I had plenty of uncles and aunts and subsequent cousins. There were many friends and acquaintances about too and with the closeness of

4

village life these people brought a sense of involvement and fulfilment. It was unfortunate I never knew any of my grandparents because they had died before I was born or shortly after. My father's parents were George Samuel Elleray (died 30th January 1924) aged 50 and Agnes Jane Elleray (died 19th March 1942) and they had had a greengrocer's shop at 6 Soutergate, Ulverston. I think his father had been a joiner.

The very early years of my life I cannot comment on. First of all I wasn't in a position to remember and what I do is fuzzy and condensed, but bringing up twins in the early years of the war must have been both worrying and demanding for both my parents, and on reflection my mother did not get the true recognition for her diligence and steadiness. She was very reserved and never really argued her case forcefully but bore most of the stress involved in bringing up a family. You don't realise this until you have children of your own.

I never felt my father showed much affection towards me and neither did I expect it as I felt this was part of his role, but on occasions he was a deep influence on me, sometimes in a contradictory and dispassionate way. Although I had a sense of freedom and security throughout my childhood this was always constrained by the fear of what he would do if I went beyond the normal acceptance of what was required. His outlook and approach to life was of having no fear but this may have been due to his own temperament and experiences.

His experience in the First World War at just 18 years of age may have had a great mental and physical backlash. He had been involved with active fighting and trench warfare at Arras in France in 1918. He was decorated with the Military Medal, subsequently suffering a severe arm wound from shrapnel and the experience of a hand grenade hitting him without it going off.

In my early years my father was involved in the collection and delivery of livestock around the local area to and from different farms and to various auction marts. The furniture removal was only a small part of the business and involved moving household furniture between houses or sale rooms. There had to be a very strict procedure of cleanliness when changing from live stock to furniture. The livestock transport involved deliveries and collection from the main cattle markets in the area including Ulverston, Broughton, Millom and

Kendal. Immediately after the sale and allocation of the animals through the Ministry of Food they had to be transported for slaughter in various towns in Lancashire, particularly to the south of the county including Manchester, Liverpool, Bury, Rochdale, Bolton and Blackpool.

This committed my father to many unsociable hours. Delivering animals to go to the mart in the morning, he would have to set off to various places in south Lancashire with a full load of cattle. With a speed limit of 20 mph on the vehicle, indicated by a circular plate on the rear of the vehicle, it took over five hours to get to Manchester where he would have to unload and then return slowly home, arriving in the early hours of the following morning. He was a good provider although he was one of the old fashioned school – he was the bread-winner and expected all the domestic luxuries in return.

His outside interests were in country pursuits which included foxhunting, hound trailing and favoured blood sports. On occasions he would put two of his game cocks down to fight in the yard at Bank End were he kept the odd pig, dogs and hens. It was my duty at a young age to collect household vegetable waste, including potato peelings, cabbage leaves and carrot tops from his pals out of the village. This waste was mixed with pig and chicken meal to feed the respective animals and fowl. I went along with the game cock fighting but on refection I didn't enjoy the involvement of these activities.

My father was keen on horses and it was a sad occasion when as part of his business he took show jumping horses to Cartmel Agricultural Show for Dick Thompson. While Dick was competing in an event in the arena one of his horses fell and broke its leg and as is custom had to be shot there and then, as there was no alternative. This shooting was carried out by a veterinary surgeon in the woods, directly behind my father's cattle truck, and my father held the horse while it was shot. He asked me to move away whilst it happened. Although he presented a hard approach he broke down after the shooting.

He was interested in sport in general and supported the local rugby league team at Craven Park in Barrow and he used to take me to the games there from when I was very young. I remember the first time I went I asked him if it was real; I couldn't comprehend how full grown men could knock so much out of each other. I remember seeing such outstanding players as Willie Horne, Jim Lewthwaite, Frank Castle and Phil Jackson who all played at international level and who showed individual flare and team spirit. There was Frank Longman too, whose day job was to collect insurance money, which he did on his bike around the local villages.

I was fortunate to have the opportunity in 1951 to be taken by my father on a specially chartered steam train to London to attend the Rugby League Challenge Cup final at Wembley Stadium between Barrow and Wigan. Barrow lost 10 points to 2. Our journey took just over 24 hours. We started out early on the Saturday morning from Ulverston railway station to catch the special train setting off at Barrow, and we returned on Sunday afternoon.

My mother's social life involved attending local village activities including whist drives and Mothers Union meetings which she usually went to with her sister-in-law, Edith Shuttleworth, wife of her eldest brother William who lived in the end house at Craglands, No 6. Other than this she was a homely person who carried out her duties in a calm and professional manner and many times must have been provoked by the temperament of my father and her twins' testing of her patience.

These were post-war years and everything was on ration. We had special ration books containing unit coupons for each item. You were allowed so many for clothes, others for food through your butcher or grocer. The coupons indicated how much you were allowed to buy in the way of sugar, bacon, cheese, fats, eggs, meat, tea and sweets (see Appendix E) My mother was very methodical and each week Mr Taylor who, as the representative of Parkers, the Grocers in Ulverston, would deliver her order and take away a list for the following week. He would read the list through, and after each item listed he would go "yip" in acknowledgement and confirming the item. One of these lists ended up in the Record Office in Barrow-in-Furness as a typical grocery list with the respective prices for a family in the late 1940s. I don't know how it got there but it was brought to my attention in the 1990s by a neighbour who was doing some research on another subject.

Many studies have been carried out regarding twins, but my sister and I are not identical and as time went on we became individuals with virtually opposite attributes and mannerisms. Despite the fact we were brought up in exactly the same environment, our natures and characteristics are completely different – how we think and behave, our attitude to life, our differences in health and education. Having said that, we never have arguments and very few conflicts. We don't live in each others pockets but have great respect and pride for each other.

This leads me on to pre-school years, which I have little recollection of but know something about from various comments by uncles and aunts. We were kids who played our mother up and caused a lot of noise. My mother was slightly deaf and she did not hear everything that was going on.

One of the earliest recollections I have was of being taken down to the farm opposite the Derby Arms. It was a threshing day and the thresher was driven by a steam traction engine owned and run by Edward Garnett whose relation were also farmers in the village. The steam engine was driven to various local farms to provide them with a day or two's threshing. The thresher was belt driven from the steam engine and separated the grain from the stalks, and then the chaff, or outer shell, from the grain. This process was very dusty and with all the flapping of belts and noise, and vermin scurrying about, it wasn't a very pleasant place to be. On that occasion I was allowed to operate the lever to engage the whistle by reaching it from my father's shoulder.

In the early years on our birthday "Auntie" Peggy, not our real auntie, cycled from her home at Hill Top, Greenodd, to visit it us. Peggy was the daughter of Charlie Rodgers, a friend of my father's who was associated with the butcher and the slaughter of animals through the Barrow Cooperative. On my father's death in 1984 the only thing Peggy enquired and asked for was the cast iron boiler out of the washhouse; she had a use for it at Hilltop. Peggy had remembered this as being in place in the 1940s. I dismantled it and took it to her. She gave me a beautiful Lakeland stone lamp for my troubles.

Our birthday presents tended to be combined with Christmas presents and we received the basic stocking fillers and book annuals, and I usually got a Meccano set, starting from the basic one and building up to the more complicated ones with each passing year. I enjoyed making up the things in the catalogue such as cars and cranes and bridges. All the pieces fitted together using nuts and bolts and washers and you even got a spring-operated clockwork motor in the later sets which allowed you to operate your cranes and vehicles.

Our method of getting to places as babies was in a large twin pram. On sunny occasions we were installed in it and wheeled into the garden with the two hoods angled back. Our other form of transport was in the cab of the cattle truck belonging to my father. Often our feet were surrounded by halters which would be attached around the cows' heads to walk them and control them when entering or leaving the truck. There was usually a couple of sheep dogs amongst our legs too,which my father had for herding and controlling stock.

On social visits and Sunday afternoon trips I recall visiting Bardsea and Goadsbarrow beaches but generally my father would take us to where he was travelling as part of his business which could be anywhere in the north of England. The cattle truck was also used for visits to the hospital or the doctor. On one occasion I had to be taken to Dr Boyd's surgery in Ulverston opposite the Palladium Cinema which is now the bus stand in Victoria Road. I had cut my right eyebrow after pushing my sister's doll's pram out of the way when it tipped up and I hit my eyebrow on the sharp corner of the square table leg. It was duly stitched up by Dr Boyd whilst I sat on my father's knee. I can visualise and feel the needle going in to this day and the scar on my eyebrow remains with me. The guilty table leg, the one nearest the door, was covered by an old sock to cushion against further incidents; the nearest thing my father got to a Health and Safety Policy.

Visits to the doctor were not that frequent. We had our incidents of contagious diseases such as measles, chickenpox and impetigo and must have had reoccurring throat problem because we had our tonsils removed in what I thought were barbaric conditions in Ulverston Cottage Hospital. Another time I had to attend the doctor when I swallowed an old 12-sided three penny coin, known as the three-penny-bit, the yellow one with angular sides.

The doctor insisted I did my toiletry into a chamber pot and to inspect each time to see if the coin had passed through, and in due course it was duly delivered, slightly tarnished but still valuable and legal tender.

In the mid-1940s few households had private telephones but people had access to public telephone boxes which were painted red and there was one in the village adjacent to the Low Midtown farm wall and at the junction with the Derby Arms and Bankfield Hall. My father decided to have a telephone for his business which was virtually essential. He told me about this and I said, "where are you going to put it?" He said, "On the window ledge." Puzzled, I said, "How? It won't fit in there", because to me a telephone included the ubiquitous red box identified in large letters as "Telephone". How words and impression convey different images of reality. The telephone number was Bardsea 237.

The telephone was an important tool. Previously communication had to be made by word of mouth or even on a written postcard. In some cases the telephone was not the most suitable method. If calves had been born during the night and the farmers wanted their immediate delivery to the auction, they would signal this by tying a rag to the roadside signpost to their farm which indicated to my father a calf or some animal needed immediate delivery to auction. I remember this particularly happening on the farms between Broughton and Millom for delivery on a Monday morning to Millom Auction Mart.

One day when I was about ten I must have pleased my father. After helping load and discharge sheep at various farms, he offered to buy me a book of my choice. On completion of the work he took me to Atkinson's, a well-established bookshop near the market square in Ulverston. I selected a small compact hardback book, *Scott of the Antarctic*. The cover had a pastel blue background with Scott positioned left-of-centre with his ice axe and exploring equipment. I enjoyed the story of Scott and his journey to the South Pole and always valued this book.

Some of the people who assisted my father as helpers, especially around the auction marts, were usually involved with casual work.

There was one helper from Ulverston who my father relied on who was deaf and dumb. On occasions when my father called in at home he would bring him in for tea and snacks. My support for him was by understanding as he tried to explain things with various sounds and gestures. I never felt uncomfortable in this situation and was impressed by how well he integrated into society.

Starting School

My formal education started at Urswick Grammar School on the 17th January 1944. Admission No 2414 (my sister was No. 2415), aged five years and one month. The school was situated in Little Urswick, set back off the road beyond the school green which was on a steep, undulating slope to the school. It was a church school dating back to 13th March 1585 and carried the name Grammar from its previous times. At the time of me starting school it catered for scholars up to their time of leaving education at age 15, but by the time I was due to leave it was at 11 years of age. The Education Act of 1944 stated primary and secondary education had to be separate. If you passed the 11-plus examination you then went on to Grammar school and if you failed you went to the Secondary Modern, both in Ulverston, although students who lived in the Stainton area went on to Dowdales Secondary Modern School in Dalton if they failed the 11-plus.

The school was situated on a large piece of rough, craggy ground, probably 100 yards long, that went to the road and was unfenced. To the north side of the school was private property including the home of Mr Bibby and some out-buildings belonging to a nearby farm. To the other side was the schoolhouse which was adjoined to the school, and a few yards farther on was The Swan public house where Johnnie Fay was the landlord and pianist. These enclosed the play area and we all knew the limits of where we could go and not go, and I never remember property being trespassed or damaged. With the school green being completely open we were like hefted sheep and remained within our territory.

The building consisted of three classes: bottom, middle and top, and within these there was a limited amount of streaming – e.g. Standard 1 and Standard 2 – and they catered for all abilities. There was always a friendly atmosphere with good pupil cooperation, interest and participation. In the early years there are few clues for which direction each child would take, but at the end of our time there certain characteristics were forming. There were individuals with good practical skills, or good memory; some had mathematical talents, or were good at poetry reciting and yet others with practical joking skills. Being a village school there was a strong bias towards rural and country skills.

The teaching staff at the start were the headmaster Mr Swainson, Miss Lumb, Miss Turney, and Miss Taylor. Mr Swainson was replaced by Miss Pixton who was later replaced by Miss Dobson. Miss Dobson was part of a local family and lived in one of the stone terraced houses – "North view" on the left-hand side between the junction to Little Urswick and Hooks Lane (the quarry) and the school. It was with some sort of respect that we would call for her on our way to school, and she would ask us to wait in the hall while she finished preparing herself for the day. Her father, John, had previously been the headmaster of the school and when he was to be buried he requested to be buried under the Church wall adjacent to the road that leads from Great Urswick to the school so that he could hear the children walking to school.

It was customary to walk to and from school, which was a mile each way. In the early days my mother would escort us on her bicycle, and she would also bring our lunches at dinner time. Eventually the walking to and from school became a group activity with the Slater family who lived directly opposite to us. That family consisted of six children with five going to school at one time. We would collect other friends and school mates on the way too. The return journey in the afternoon would be with a group of fellow pupils.

The one-mile walk was sometimes a stroll or dawdle with slow progress but I don't think we were ever late for school. A slow pace may have been more common on the way home, with all the distractions. The road meandered and passed sites of village life, farm entrances usually covered by cow dung, grass and hay seeds, as well as gardens, orchards, a stately home, pubs, the village shop, the church and the tarns. The main tarn is approximately a quarter mile long and an eighth wide. There were two smaller tarns, one in the field opposite the vicarage, called "Scriflates", and the other situated in the field between the recreation hall and Hooks Lane. Over the years both of these were filled in following accidental deaths but in periods of heavy rainfall water still collects there.

In winter these smaller tarns froze over and produced excellent skating facilities and in the winter of 1947 the main tarn froze over too. The flood water in the field between Holme Bank farm and the tarn, where Gleaston Beck runs south out of the tarn, quite frequently froze and was a popular place to play ice hockey. Some of us had ice skates, and we played with sticks and a piece of wood for the puck. This relatively small piece of frozen water catered for people of all ages as well as small children. I remember "Pop", the girlfriend and subsequently the wife of Tom Postlethwaite, the farmer's son from Holme Bank. Although she would have been some years older than me, she joined in and took an active part, and she had very impressive skating legs and dressed appropriately though very disconcertingly for young adolescent males.

The walk to and from school was a rich experience in itself. It offered lessons in the harmony and ways of the nature around us, between the buildings and tarns, in fields, trees and hedgerows. One thing we would do on our way was chat with the roadmen who cleaned and maintained the sides of the road with their sickle, and their piece of stick for control. A major talking point was when they resurfaced the road with boiling tar and chippings. This always created interest as the tar was heated and, when boiling, spread over the road and then stone chippings were shovelled onto it from heaps aligned at equidistance on the roadside. The men always wore protective legging and boots but were nonetheless splattered with a tarry mess. After a time, the excess, small angular chippings which were loose on the surface were swept up and gathered to be made use of at another section of the road.

The Slater family lived opposite to us in a row of four terraced houses, known as Tinkers' Row, which was set into a steep bank and fronted directly onto the road. Today it has been modernised and forms one complete single house. The houses did not have electricity or running water and the earthen toilets were at the rear of the house in a very steep garden, which went the full length of the terrace and was so steep that when digging it appeared your nose was touching the ground in front.

In our house we had all the current modern facilities, and the Slater boys where fascinated and intrigued by the light switches and how they could turn lights on and off. Water was collected by them for family and domestic use from a pump situated in a pump house about 20 yards from the house and positioned in the side of the banking opposite the larger terraced houses known as Gorden Terrace. At the one end of this terrace was the police station and at the other lived Mr and Mrs Varcoe, whose son Tony was a close friend of mine in my early school years. He was a keen footballer and collected sports cuttings out of the newspapers and between us we used to compile scrap books of these cutting using "Gloy" paste, basically flour and water, to secure them.

Mr and Mrs Slater raised six children – five boys and one girl – in what today you would call cramped conditions. The sleeping arrangements were head to toe. Their aunties lived at the other end of the terrace with a space in between which was a house used for storage. They were a very close family and operated as a unit under the administration of Mrs (Mary) Slater whose character and domestic skills had the place running like a well-oiled machine. At one time she had a whistle to blow for meal times which could be heard in the surrounding fields where we might be playing. Mr (Frank) Slater provided fatherly support, covering all outside activities. The Slater family played a very large part in my early years and even more so in the later years when the eldest son, Alan, married my twin sister.

In my early school years I was directly under the influence, direction and supervision of my parents, supportive uncles and aunts as well as my teachers. My first school teacher (Class 1) was Miss Lumb who I vaguely remember and who was followed quickly by Miss Turney who always looked very tall to me. She had a distinct clarity of voice and wore glasses and bright red lipstick that contrasted memorably with her white teeth. This image may have been distorted because I was looking from a sitting position while she tended to teach standing up above us. Her ginger hair was also a strong feature. She was the one who introduced me to the basics of reading and writing. Reading was taught through the "Mr and Mrs Peg" books, and the writing and formation of letters on a blackboard set on an easel. The classroom was heated by a coke stove situated in the middle at the front of the class. On some occasions just after the stoves had been lit and the wind was in the wrong direction they produced so much smoke that some mornings we were not allowed in until the fumes had cleared. Another problem was when the base and local areas of the stove would glow bright red with the excessive heat.

Miss Turney, now called Joyce Parke, lives in Ulverston and I frequently talk to her and we reminisce, and she is always interested in my family and my school colleagues. She still has a clarity of voice and excellent diction and command of the English language. She was one of my teachers that most impressed me, perhaps because she was one of the first, but on reflection she had good teaching qualities too. I once reported Stan Fisher to her for having his eyes open when saying prayers. We all should have our eyes shut and our hands clasped in the praying position. Miss Turney said, "How did you know they were open if your eyes were shut?"

My teacher in Class 2 (Middle class) was Miss Taylor and she became Mrs Birkett during my time at the school. She was an industrious teacher, but never seemed to have a big influence on me. Perhaps it happened without my noticing it. One incident that is brought to mind is when we were singing in class and she stopped the singing and asked, "Who is it making that *noise*?" There was a silence, and after a slight pause everybody was pointing at me. I felt embarrassed and uncomfortable because I didn't know I was making a noise. Perhaps it may have been in the wrong key for me, and one of my regrets since then is not being able to sing in tune. Some people have a natural ability which I never had and I always get an uncomfortable feeling and lack confidence when singing in a group or community setting, and I would never attempt a solo. This may be due to that incident!

The class teacher in the Class 3 (Top class) was Miss Helena Dobson. She was also the headmistress. It was in this class that I developed an interest in learning. I suppose in any child's education this is the time that things are coming together, after having acquired basics skills in reading, writing and multiplication and long division and also in drawing and painting. Once I did a pencil shading drawing of an otter overlooking a semi-submerged stone in water. I portrayed the otter with beautiful smooth curves and protruding whiskers, which I was quite proud of. I felt such factors, along with the friendly atmosphere, helped me to have an enquiring and curious mind.

Miss Dobson was strict about discipline and insisted that good English was spoken and written. This was often a problem to me and other scholars having been brought up in a village and used to local dialect and slang. It was part of our environment and built into our genes, though people in the family tried occasionally to correct it, but it was our natural way of speaking.

In one incident I was asked in front of the class by Miss Dobson to explain what I had been doing in the holidays and I mentioned I had been to the "abitires" in Barrow with my father to deliver some cattle for slaughter. She reminded me that the name was "abattoir", pronounced ab-uh-twar, derived from the French word for "to fell".

Miss Dobson was very interested in promoting the countryside and nature. She encouraged our interest in things that were going on around us. Although I was interested I was never enthusiastic about knowing all the wild flowers names, and this was reported in one of my annual school reports (see Appendix C). In one gardening lesson in the school garden at the rear of the school Mr Pierpoint the class teacher was explaining the parts of flowers and plants when a strong breeze got up. I asked, "Sir, where does the wind come from?" He explained it was due to the differences in air pressure and when the air moves from a high pressure to a lower pressure. This is what I was more interested in.

Miss Dobson's interest in natural things was shown in the way we had to report once a week during the relevant lesson on such things as items of weather, wind direction, maxium and minimum temperature, rainfall and all other items of interest experienced by the scholars during the week.

This was my first formal introduction to presenting information in tabular, symbolic and written form to establish a complete, overall picture quickly. This became very valuable later in life, especially in communicating and presenting information (see Appendix D). I was at ease with representing facts and information plainly and to the point. Perhaps I was unmotivated or too lazy to try to reply in a creative or verbose and indirect manner.

The constraints of learning both at school and at home were regulated by access to reading, chalk and talk, teacher's discussions, the library and the occasional radio programme. The learning was by rote and absorbing information presented to us. There was little scope for expressing oneself in ways outside the teacher's approach.

I was fairly good at absorbing facts and reasoning but not always able to think much outside the views being taught and I had little propensity for creative writing. I was always interested in reading and had access to daily, evening, and weekend papers. I also enjoyed reading the Biggles series of books written by Captain W. E. Johns, which were about the adventures of aircraft pilot Biggles in the 1920s. and the *Adventures of Tom Sawyer* and *Huckleberry Finn*, by Mark Twain.

A visit by the school dentist during one of his periodic checks made me think on my feet when he asked me how often I cleaned my teeth. I replied, "Every Thursday." "Why every Thursday?" he asked. I had to think quickly and I said because it was market day.

Miss Dobson had a discoloured, piebald right eye which sometimes became a distraction, especially when you came into face-to-face contact when she was doubting and questioning you. She also had an affinity for long-sleeved, unfashionable cardigans.

Children in the class included Joan Hinchy who lived just across the road from school and who had a brilliant memory for poetry. Her father, Sam, was the verger for the church and caretaker for the adjacent Sunday school premises. He was a beautiful yodeller and he gave many repertoires while going about his work. Lily Postlethwaite was a small, dark-haired girl from Stainton who sat in front of me in the top class and who had a large plait of hair. June Stamford was a pleasant girl who always wore her hair in a pair of plaits. Audrey Goodall was a very nice, reserved girl who always appeared to wear fair Isle jumpers. The Fisher brothers, Brian and Stan, who came from Skeldon Moor, were keen on country sports and contributed to nature study lessons with details of what they had seen and got up to. Some of their stories were obviously exaggerated for effect but there was a lot of substance behind them too. Brian Lambert came from Stainton and he was always interested in mechanical toys and trains. Ray Braithwaite came from Stainton too; he was stocky and strong, but in any combat games I considered myself a match! Brian Hurford lived directly opposite the school in the Post Office. Brian was a deep thinker and wore very thick lenses in his glasses and after working as an agricultural engineer became a very successful farmer in the Penrith area. Brian and I both sent away independently for the John Player 1948/1949 annuals on cricket and football which provided all the scores and team statistics for the year. We both had an interest in comparing the statistics, analysing how each team player had performed over the season. Leslie Chapman (Chappie) was a farmer's son whose father Arthur farmed a few yards away from the school. June Latimer was a lovely girl who lived in an end-of-terrace house at Brow End, overlooking the tarn. She had a younger brother Douglas who was also interested in mechanical toys and who eventually owned his own garage business. Jimmy Steel (Loftie) was a tall, lean and unpredictable lad who was full of energy and boyish pranks. James Pattinson had a lazy eye and the other lens of his glasses was covered to correct this. His father, Dud, was a quarryman at Stainton Quarry, and he lived in the small terraced cottages opposite the tarn and adjacent to the shop and General Burgoyne. Norman, Jean and Sheila Hudson lived in a cottage up the lane known as Brow Edge. Their father, Bill, was an authority on valve radios which were the 'in' thing at the time, pre-television. Norman was the envy of us all when he got a job at 15 at a cinema in Barrow as a projectionist and thus had access to all the films, which was a privileged position in what was becoming a popular entertainment activity. There was also Brenda Courtney, whose father, Harry, ran the village shop.

During and towards the end of my primary school period I became an active member of the cub scouts and later the scouts. These were initiated by Rev. Malcolm Douglas Grieve, the Vicar of Urswick who was also a big contributor to the church school and a lot of associated activities involving the church, the school and village life.

Mr Grieve came to the parish directly after the aftermath of war and had a vision to help the youth. Although classed as "high" church he had a sincere interest in the parish and its inhabitants. He was helped in setting up the scout group by Irving Gowling who was my neighbour and lived with his parents in the adjoining bungalow. Mr Jack Gowling, his father, had a small Nissan-hut workshop behind his house where he used to manufacture and build small steam engines. In the front room of the house he had a model of the Queen Mary which was about 2–3 foot long, which he'd built with his own hands.

The church and its associated activities provided a core base and encompassed the theme of village life for me and many other children. In my early years it was conventional to attend Sunday school where Joan Wood was the teacher and pianist. Her playing "By Cool Siloam's Shady Rill", the Rushbearing hymn, on the Sunday school piano always appealed to me and I still talk to Joan about it today, and she never fails to remind me she remembers me being born. She lived next door in the very early years of my life.

We all took part in the annual Rushbearing event which occurs on St Michael's Day, the Sunday nearest the 29th September. The event involved the gathering of rushes and carrying them in a formal procession from the school at Little Urswick to the bottom of Daisy Hill in Great Urswick and back to the church for the service, during which the bundles of rushes were laid on the church floor which in much earlier days was earthen and the rushes provided some warmth in the winter months. The procession was led by a person carrying a large banner along with the annually elected Rushbearing Queen chosen from the girls in the village, and boys known as the sword-bearers carried swords. I didn't attend Sunday school out of choice but more because of parent and peer pressure, but once there it was a good social get-together.

By the time I was ten in my own mind I had limited opinions and judgement. These were providing me with some sort of understand-ing of the tangible structures of pecking orders, of my relationship to my parents, sister, uncles, aunts, friends and my parents' colleagues.

I was able to make comparisons between myself and my sister, between my friends and her friends and appreciate the age difference with my parents. At that age parents always appeared wise and old and you didn't doubt their sincerity but accepted what they said and did as they told without question. I felt in many issues I had the edge on my sister on the way I conducted myself in a controlled manner whereas she would perhaps be a bit more unpredictable in her behaviour.

At the time I joined the cub scouts my sister joined the brownies. Both these events took place in the Sunday school, which was a small, detached building just outside the grounds of the Church and which had adequate floor space for young people to be active in games and more serious exercises. The school overlooks the war memorial and the area which is now known as Kirk Flat housing estate. Social events also took place in the Sunday school. Other social gatherings took place in the Recreation Hall which is between the church and the old Grammar school in Little Urswick. This was a much larger building than the Sunday school and was built in 1929 by the villagers on land donated by a local farmer, George Stables, and was constructed with second-hand bricks from Lowfield Mine Chimney. It had the peculiarity of being a rectangular building made out of curved bricks. It catered for larger social events for the surrounding villages.

Another small social gathering place was the "Reading Room" above Harry Stables' building material storage space up Neales Row. This was for much older people and was used by them for playing cards, crib, and billiards, and the playing of the odd gramophone and radio was permitted too. This area of Neales Row housed a lot of my friends and contacts including the Steels – Alan, Jean and Jimmy; the Fitzgeralds – Maurice and Rita; the Halls – Deason; the Marshals – Gordon, Joyce, Jean and Olive. With so many children in the locality it became an attractive play arena for children. To get there you had to turn off the road and up an incline to Neales Row and then passed Miss Hool's house, called "Neale House", which faced onto the main road and adjacent to the slope. When any ball games were played at the flat area at the top the ball would roll down and often bump up against her back door. On one occasion she took the small ball and

20

wouldn't return it and I think it belonged to a small boy, Barry Fitzgerald, and Mr Fitzgerald became involved and went to see Miss Hool but she refused to hand the ball over, at which point Mr Fitzgerald turned 90 degrees and put his fist through one of her small paned windows.

Play both at school and after school occupied a large amount of time and was on most occasions rewarding and enjoyable but on others the situation often became heated involving rows, taking sides and fighting to defend yourself or friends. Situations soon got resolved and play went on but perhaps in different groups which then only lasted a few days. Then, as today, there was a certain amount of bullying but this was part of setting the stall out on how to defend yourself. The only time I experienced bullying was with a boy who was a few years older than me and a lot stronger. He was a farmer's son and original lived in the village, but they moved to a farm on the road from High Carley Sanatorium to Lindal, known as Green Lane. He used his uncouth attitude and physical strength to get his own way and upset me, and one time I went crying into my house. My father immediately told me to get out there and stick up for myself. That is easier said than done and there was no way I could physically compete with the boy. Having said that, these were isolated incidents and play went on as normal.

Some other games and play activity included "Stick a Rodger" which was a game with two teams where you had somebody standing up straight with their back against the wall for support and the rest of the team bent over in a line at 90 degrees with the first head in the stomach of the person standing and the rest with their heads in the crotch of the one before, like a rugby scrum but in a line. The other team had to individually take turn to jump up and over the hunched line and land as far forward on the stooped backs as possible until as many as the team had managed to leap up there. When everyone of the team was on safely and securely you shouted "Stick a Rodger!"

One of the more dangerous games was the one we used to play on the school green called "British Bulldog" where a tall boy would have a smaller boy sitting on his shoulders and another pair would challenge to see who could pull the other one off first. With me being small I was the one on the shoulders and took the knocks when hitting the ground.

Other games included marbles, which were played by gouging a small hole in the ground with the heel of your shoe and then rolling the marble, usually made of glass but others were made from a ceramic type material, into it. An arbitrary distance was established from the hole for rolling the marbles from, and the players would take it in turns and the winner would collect all the marbles in the hole. Then there was "whip-and-top" in which an inverted, conically shaped piece of wood was spun round by means of a leather or string whip which was then used to control and move the top around by further lashing of the whip. The top had a small groove for this purpose. We also played hopscotch, tin can "orky", and also "booly" which involved steering a moving steel hoop with a hook with which you made contact with the hoop and propelled it forward.

Football was played usually with a small ball but on occasions with a blown-up pig's bladder. The area of the road between our house and the Slater's was cordoned off by placing an item of clothing at the four corners to indicate the length of the designated area and also the width of the goal. Bearing in mind that a common form of footwear at the time was clogs with metal caulkers, football became a dangerous pastime. One of the Slater boys, Frank, had the ability to strike the ball from any place on his clog. He appeared to be able to twist and revolve his ankle at the ball and quite often a player would be struck by any part of his clog. For this reason he was called "Shin-tapper-Shinty".

The other popular place for football was the area embracing the frontage of Bankfield. This was a much bigger area and could accommodate numerous people of different ages. Although it was classed as illegal to play ball games in the road the village policeman, Bob May, had a sympathetic approach and only acted when it became too dangerous to property and road safety. Football was very popular throughout all seasons and local village children played officially arranged matches against adjacent villages. At one match the referee, Alf Whalley, called me "Eight-Goal Elleray" after I scored eight goals against his local team, Leece. I was referred to sometimes as "lile Ernie" after my father, and also "lile blackie" and later on in life, in some talk hidden from me, as the "little black monkey", possibly because of my strong eyebrows and hairy body, even to my finger tips.

Other areas of play included Birkrigg Common, for its wide open spaces and disused small quarry, Skelemore Head and the craggy ground behind Neales row was used for its rugged terrain for playing cowboys and Indians. These activities were acted out with great imagination with imitation guns and home-made bows made of birch tree cuttings and string, and with arrows made from straight pieces of stick out of the hedges which had to be adapted by having a point at one end and a small nick at the other to fit onto the string.

One summertime activity was when whole families walked out of Urswick up the road to Birkrigg Common and over "Green Pad" to Bardsea. The grass pathway was a direct route over the top of Birkrigg Common, down the other side, past the stone circle, and by Sea Wood. Eventually we arrived on the shore and picnicked behind a large boulder and swam in the sea. The return journey always seemed long to us because we had spent our energies on the beach, but we overcame this with games along the way and the time soon passed.

An easy access play area from my home was the field known as "Old Toe" which was the name of the field a few yards up the road from us, and a few yards further north was Flat Wood, at the time called "Loving Lizzie's wood" – not her proper name – because she lived in the bungalow on the edge of the wood and kept hens and animals in the house. We climbed trees and played games in the wood, usually on our way to Skelmore Head. On the way home my sister would pick the snowdrops and daffodils in early spring and blue bells and primroses in summer in and near the wood.

In winter we made use of the hills on Birkrigg Common for adventures and sledging, especially on the slope known as "The Hag" which was adjacent to the road to Birkrigg Common and the one to Holme Bank. The gradient was such it was possible to cross the road onto an area known as "The Landing" and nearly reach the tarn. This was also the area where the annual bonfire was made. Sledges varied in all forms. Some were just a series of pieces of wood. The body of mine, which was built by my cousin's husband who had a fabrication/engineering business in south Ulverston, was made of old inch wood, and the runners and foot rests of thick angle iron. It was far too heavy to be speedy but when it got up speed it was a lethal machine.

We spent many happy hours walking and playing around the tarn, making tracks and dens in the reed beds especially the ones on the eastern side of the tarn which was easily approached from the Landing, the smithy and hag-end houses.

We also spent many hours fishing in the tarn. The main place was the small jetty near to where the Coot Restaurant is now. On calm evenings, using just a cane, nylon line, lead sinkers, a goose-feather quill and hook, using worms, maggots or bread paste for bait, we sometimes got as many as forty catches in a night. We caught roach, bream and eels.

The only bad experience of playing around the tarn was when my mother took me at an early age for a walk which included the footpath between the Sunday school and the Hag, at the section before it meets the foot bridge over Gleaston Beck at the south end of the tarn. I must have veered off the foot path and disturbed two swans probably nesting there and one flew at me and attacked me with its wings. This was very frightening and I've always since had reservations about approaching birds – large or small – especially if they begin flapping their wings. I've even had difficulty trying to remove a small sparrow, with its flapping wings, from my garage.

One or two people who had access to the tarn had rowing boats which were used for fishing and general relaxation. One of those was Mr (Johnnie) Roe of the General Burgoyne public house who was an exponent of the British monologue. The "Lion and Albert" comes to mind. His son, Geoff, who was a couple of years older than me, used his father's boat quite frequently. On one occasion I and a couple of other young lads followed him by swimming behind the boat. We went from his base across to Harry Wood's farm opposite, a very dangerous thing to do but we got away with it. It was some achievement but it could have gone so badly wrong.

Geoff was also a good pianist and accordion player and when the pub was quiet I used to join him around the piano. He loaned me the *News Chronical* hard-backed music book at the time and I have still got it to this day. He was an expert card player and practiced his art on the school bus home and when he was an apprentice at Vickers he was known as the top card player of one of the decks – no pun intended – of the luxury liner under construction.

He became the licensee of the pub on his father's death and used the slogan "The pies are lovely tonight" to promote sales.

The smithy was also a good meeting place where Jimmy Newby the blacksmith used to shoe horses on a regular basis, having to heat the shoes to a high temperature in a coke fire which had to be energised by hand bellows, and then the shoe was shaped and drilled over the anvil and then burnt onto the hoof, and I can still smell the burning flesh.

Other tradesmen, craft and business people in the area included Mr Ashburner – coachbuilder and wheelwright; Ernest Sawery – joiner and undertaker; Harold Wood – butcher with his own slaughter house; the Miss Muggletons – two sisters who ran a small wooden shop and Post Office. Across the tarn there was Len Garnet – joiner; and Harry Stables and Mr Stubbs – builders. All these people were on good terms with us and would always have time to talk and to show us what they were doing. The slaughter house of Harold Wood received a lot of attention because of its activities. On one occasion I remember a cow being transported from Little Urswick on a sledge towed behind a tractor. The animal had keeled over with grass staggers, a symptom of eating too much young grass. It was fastened on its back onto the sledge with its bloated stomach and the four legs pointing up to the sky. On arrival at the slaughter house, John Stephenson, the butcher at the time, just pricked its stomach with his knife and a large spray of grass sludge hit the ceiling which must have been thirty foot up.... Some pressure!

The village also had an intake of evacuees from the Salford area of Manchester who were allocated to certain houses and hosts in the village although I only have a vague memory of them. They were accepted into village life and they were involved in the spirit of the village, although there may have been one or two villagers who would not accept as part of us but they were in the minority.

Towards the late 1940s the big house of Bankfield was converted into a convalescent home for boys from Liverpool and Merseyside. Mr Ratty, who was in charge of the home, used to arrange football and sporting events with the boys of the village. They had a beautiful lawn and a proper football field with nets and goal posts. The field was between Bankfield and Bank End. There were oranges and a cup of cocoa at half time served from a hatch at the side of the house. We always had the advantage of being stronger and we would go in for the kill, sometimes winning by as much as eleven goals, but it provided the activities that the boys needed.

Other playmates were Bill and George Woodall whose parents lived at Causey Wood, a large house on a smallholding which was up the road and left into Stone Dike Lane. Their father was a butcher and had a business in Barrow on the corner of Lumley and Smeaton streets. Our families were friends and we enjoyed their company on social events and at Christmas time. They also had cousins who used to visit: John, Brian and Joan Richmond, whose parents had the Post Office which formed part or their house in Leece. Including my sister we formed a compact group when playing in the grounds of Causey Wood.

It was the Woodalls that introduced us to one of several family holidays in Blackpool at a B&B belonging to Mrs Walters in a street off Talbot Road. These were enjoyable holidays. We stayed for a week and enjoyed all the variety shows, the Tower, and the Tower circus as well as the not so pleasant trips to Fleetwood market which I found uneventful. Other enjoyable day trips were to Blackpool and Morecambe illuminations in September/October, to Southport flower show which was always around my mother's birthday on the 25th August, and Chester was a popular destination too. Many of these day trips were organised by Hadwin's Coaches in Ulverston.

The area around Bank End was a source of play, work and village culture. One section adjacent to the barn was used as a dolls' house where my cousin Myra, who was a few years older than me, used to play. In there was a sea shell which if you put it to your ear she said you could hear the tide coming in. After we tried it we believed her. Myra lived with her parents at Craglands and was the daughter of my mother's eldest brother, William Shuttleworth, and his wife, Edith.

The yard which formed the centre piece between the houses and the out-buildings gave access to the shippon and cart house which previously was used to store carts, including the carts of a local butcher, William Slater, a stick house and pig sty.

The cart house was the main store for my father's equipment and tools and there was always a 50-gallon oil drum with a brass pumping arrangement that allowed you to draw off a pint or a quart or whatever was required. I still have this brass pump. It's 42 inches high and an inch and a quarter in diameter and it is polished up beautifully and quite a pleasant piece to display. The drum used to be topped up with "Ovaline" by Brett's Oil, and the local representative was a Mr Hughes who lived in the area around Holme Bank. He was a sergeant-major type of chap with an air of superiority but obviously he knew how to sell oil. He was a drinking pal of my father's and in those days it would be considered as networking for business and keeping your customers happy. One of the spin-offs of this was we used to get a small, daily tear-off calendar each year from Bretts with the date indicated by a prominent red coloured number and a little slogan on the bottom on each page. It was fascinating as a child to tear off the pages as each day went by and there was sometimes a tussle between my sister and I about who's turn it was to do it.

The gardens at Bank End were maintained by Mr Lindsey from out of the village. He had a substantial handcart which he used to transport all his gardening equipment, but he was quite elderly and he used to perspire and mucus would drip off the end of his nose which he would wipe with a dirty handkerchief. This handcart was quite valuable to us because he used to allow us to use it to collect material for the annual Guy Fawkes celebration bonfire. We would collect bracken off Birkrigg Common and bring it down to the edge of the tarn where the bonfire was constructed. On one or two occasions we may have broken a shaft or leg which he was not pleased about, but he always forgave us. The only other person I remember with a handcart was Harry Courtney who was the proprietor of the village shop. Every Monday he used to stock up his cart with consumables, cover it over with a waterproof cover and push it to High Carley Sanatorium for patients. This would be a good mile each way but this cart was more streamlined than the one Mr Lindsay had and had rubber tyres.

Gardening in those days, directly after the war, and with shortages of vegetables and fruit, was important, and any spare land was used to produce vegetables. I remember my father let Mr Oldcorn cultivate and produce vegetables in the plot in front of our house. Mr Oldcorn was called "Peg Leg" because he only had one leg but he managed to garden and get about with the aid of a crutch. In fact he could garden as well as any full-limbed person and it was interesting to watch how he dug the garden over with his fork and used his crutch for balancing and then how he rode his bike with the crutch attached to the cross bar, powering the bike with one foot. My father cultivated the area adjacent to the house to grow spring onions, potatoes, sprouts and cabbages. There were also blackcurrent trees and an area of grass where we had hens in a coup.

At Bank End Reuben Stables had use of the farm buildings including the shippon, and the barn directly above, where he milked his herd consisting of about 6 to 8 milk cows, including a Jersey. He milked these cows by hand, seated on a three-legged stool and wearing his cap back to front with his forehead pressed against the cow's belly. He delivered the milk fresh to local people including my mother and father and continued to do so until about 1954. My father used to help him bring in his new-mown hay from the fields by using his cattle truck. The only other means was by horse and cart, which Reuben also used. Reuben's son Harry, who was a builder, housed his truck in the area next to the shippon which was the old covered in midden (see Appendix F2).

My parents, my sister and I had a good neighbourly relationship with the residents of Bank End, who included Mr and Mrs Moralee, Mr Braithwaite, Auntie Cissy and Mrs Helm. Mrs Moralee's daughter, Doris Sansom, was married to the Vickers Armstongs Ltd industrial photographer, Leslie Sansom. They lived in London because Leslie was moved to head offices in London but they used to travel up to see her mother at least every summer. And if we were playing about in the yard at Bank End he used to whip us off to Bardsea shore and take photographs of us at play. He was a brilliant photographer and became the head photographer at Vickers Ltd. They had a son John. Doris and Leslie had an influence on me because I enjoyed the way Doris spoke so eloquently and I admired Leslie's ability to write and tell stories of his photographs; a brilliant photojournalist.

Mr Moralee died at Bank End and when my father was called in to provide help he realised immediately there was something wrong. I think my father used the old mirror test to see if he was breathing but unfortunately Mr Moralee had passed away. Mrs Helm lived in the end cottage on her own. Her son Eddie, who was married to Clarice, lived in Barrow-in-Furness but would come to see his mother at weekends.

On Saturday mornings my sister and I were taken to Ulverston by my father to a small sweet and tobacconist shop/newsagent at the bottom of the Gill in Ulverston. Miss Garnet was the proprietor. My father bought comics for me and my sister, which included *The Dandy* and *Beano,* and he would get the weekly news and a smallholder magazine. We would stay in the shop while my father did his weekly business which could involve a trip into Cases Vaults, the outlet premises of the famous Ulverston brewery at the time.

Joe Belmont, a relation of Miss Garnet, lived in Bolton in Lancashire. He was a few years older than me. I would be about 8 to 10 years old but it was his desire every summer in the school holidays to visit his relations in Ulverston purely because he wanted to travel and help my father with his work with the cattle truck. He was a cheerful lad, always whistling, and nothing was any trouble to him. It must be fifty years since I have seen him but he called in to see my sister in the summer of 2007 and I had the pleasure of meeting him again and he reminisced about the days in the cattle truck with my father.

My practical skills at this time were quite limited. I helped my father with the maintenance of his cattle truck, doing such things as renewing spark plugs, draining the water out of the radiator, cleaning out the rear of the truck onto the midden, replacing broken gates, decking and floorboards, feeding animals and gardening, and all these gave me opportunities and experiences which I should have capitalised on to make me more of a practical person but I was more a third hand in what was usually a make-do-and-mend approach sometimes lacking in craft and skill. Perhaps I would have benefited having it explained to me why these things were carried out rather than just doing them.

One of the skills I was taught in a very tutorial manner by my father was how to replace a chain and repair a puncture on a bicycle, which was quite a common problem, especially at times when farmers cut their hedges and left inviting thorns to penetrate the tyre and the inner tube. I had a cycle since I was about five years old, which at the time was a small double tubular, curved frame B.S.A. I then went onto cycles with "Sturmy Archer" three speeds. Most getting about at a young age was done by bicycle. Sometimes I used it to travel to school in Ulverston and to work in Barrow until I was about twenty.

The years at primary school lead up to the 11-plus test that decided where your future education would be.

The Butler Education Act of 1944 introduced radical changes to education where the old scholarship was replaced by a compulsory entry classification tests for all pupils. The Act was to provide secondary education for all on the principal of equality of opportunity, and it raised the school leaving age to 15. The new tripartite system offered the option of grammar, technical or secondary modern schools. The grammar school was to cater for 15–20 per cent of children with an academic curriculum leading to GCE "O" and "A" levels which prepared children for middle-class roles. The technical schools were for the "less academic" development of practical skills and preparation for skilled manual occupations. Secondary moderns were to cater for the remainder 60–70 per cent of children and were for lower ability students covering different subjects to prepare for working-class occupations.

The 11-plus test (taken at the age of 10 or 11) assessed a student's ability and intelligence and included an arithmetic and English assessment. This was a crucial time in many children's lives because it decided on what type of further education you received. From school reports, I seem to have been prone to some carelessness and laziness or lack of motivation which at the end of the day affect ability but in a lot of situations I was capable and competent.

At this age I had no concept of how this examination fitted in with the overall scheme of my education and what a milestone it could be. I remember very little of any preparation for this examination and was not conscious of any extra work for it but I think there must have been some guidance provided. There was no fast tracking and I was relying on pure natural ability.

When the results were announced and I found I had not qualified for the Grammar School I would say I was slightly disappointed but not upset by the situation. I was informed I would be attending the Victoria Secondary Modern School in Hart Street, Ulverston.

At a later date my cousins Rowland Elleray Dobson and John Elleray Park, sons of my father's sisters and slightly younger than me, passed for the Grammar School and for this achievement each were given a brand new bicycle. I suppose this offer would have been there for me if I had passed but I felt no ill feeling or jealousy over it.

This is the background from which I was launched. I had developed into a small, black-haired but athletic person never reaching more than five foot six inches in full adult life. My mind was active and I was curious not just for practical reasons but also psychologically; how people lived and behaved and what underlying factors were behind people's actions fascinated me.

I never felt I wanted to be top dog, although eager to come a close second or at least be in the frame. I probably lacked confidence and ambition and did not have an overwhelming desire to be wealthy, but on the other hand I didn't want to be poor in the sense of not being able to provide for myself.

CHAPTER TWO

1951–1955
Aged 11–16 Years
Secondary School

"The password was Paderewski"

In September 1950 I commenced my secondary education at the Ulverston Victoria Secondary Modern School off Hart Street in Ulverston which nestled under the backdrop of the Hoad and Sir John Barrow's Monument, a symbol on the landscape that can be seen from miles around.

I was placed in the 'A' stream, the top stream of a four-level academic grading system, A, B, C, and D. I had to become used to a larger class size of up to 30 pupils, all with around the same level of ability, as well as being introduced to new subjects such as French and English literature. Academically I hovered in the bottom third of the class although achieving higher positions in certain subjects – maths and science – and lower in languages and creative subjects.

The school catered for around 400 pupils and gave me the immediate feeling I was no longer to receive the individual attention I'd had at the primary village school. This was not all bad for it was a mixed sex school and increased your potential to expand your social skills to form friendships and the introduction to learning and engaging with the opposite sex. This provided a more balanced approach to adolescence and education, compared to the single-sex alternative.

I became associated with girls through the classroom lessons and activities but at play time we were segregated. In the early years at school I was informally linked with different girls through the class matchmaking process and later these relationships became more identifiable. During one break a lad said to a girl, "Are you going out with him?" – pointing to me – and she replied, "Well it's nothing to be ashamed of if I was", which did no harm to my self-esteem.

The school was a double-storey, stone building with an impressive playing field and sports facilities at the front. My form room, No 19, was housed in the wooden annex to the main building looking out onto the netball area. Although built of wood, it was warm and cosy. You were always under cover to get to the main building. My form teacher was Mr Tim Stockwell who was also my English teacher. Other rooms in the annex were rooms 17, 18 and 20. In the main building there was a large hall where morning assembly, Physical Education lessons and drama were conducted.

Most of the classrooms in the main building were decorated with heavy, dark wood and were not at all inspirational. The staircases at either end led to the office of the headmaster, Mr W. B. Walls, and adjacent to him was his deputy Mr Thornton. Along the corridor there were the needlework, library, and biology/science rooms. Behind one of these there was a small room with typewriters, which was used for commercial studies – typewriting and shorthand for pupils interested in secretarial/office work. There was also the staff room and a small office where every Monday the pupils who lived out of town had to collect their weekly bus tokens which were provided for a free public bus service from school. We travelled to school in the morning by Hadwin's coaches, a tour bus company in Ulverston.

Although small, the library at the time was considered well stocked and we also had the use of it for private study (see Appendix F1).

The school had level and spacious playing and sports fields. The main one was at the front. At the rear there was a small, concreted playground which also housed the bicycle sheds and toilets. At the other side of the school – the Hart street end – was the wooden annex which was used as the school dining room.

During my early years at the school the facilities were extended to include an adjacent area known as Ford Park, and included a large house which is now a Grade 11 listed building. It became part of the school in 1948 when Ulverston Urban District Council sold it to Lancashire County Council for that purpose. It was situated to the northeast of the school up a long drive with iron railed fences either side separating it from the large playing fields. These facilities were used for agricultural, gardening and cookery classes and the overflow lessons from the main building. It was a beautiful setting and where I had the privilege of taking my General Certificate Examination (GCE "O" level) in an environment ideal for examinations – pleasant surrounding with utmost quietness.

One of the main features of the school's setting was the backdrop of Hoad Hill and the Sir John Barrow's monument on the top. Hoad Hill was the setting for the school's cross-country races. The course started in the school field arena and out towards Ford Park, took a sharp left behind the school, up through the stiles onto an area known as "the Screws" situated at the back of Hoad, up to the monument, down the steep and rugged slope facing the town and Morecambe Bay, along Ford Park and back into the school field. One of my stronger talents was cross-country running and usually I came in the first ten, including in the inter-school races between us, the Grammar school and Dowdales Secondary Modern school in Dalton-in-Furness. This was a very strenuous run and covered steep and rugged ground. Although the winners returned in a time of around 15 minutes, it took a lot out of the pupils.

The school cross-country race was divided into a junior race for the first and second years and a senior race for the third and fourth years. When I stayed on into the new fifth form, which had been created a few years earlier, we were allowed to compete in the senior race. I thought this was unfair on the third year pupils as there was quite an age gap and difference in physical strength. My housemaster Mr Ashburner asked me why I'd declined to take part because I was expected to do well. I thought it was unfair; if I had done well I would not obtain much satisfaction and, on the other hand, if I didn't perform well I would be deflated. I just felt uneasy and didn't want to win or do well at all costs.

One of the school social events and group activity was at dinner time when school dinners were provided in a hut-type catering facility attached to the main school building. Due to numbers it was usually arranged in two sittings. I was mainly on the second sitting and we had much fun and discussion around the tables, which sat about eight, four down either side, always supervised of course. These were always hot meals including a main course and a sweet. The quality of the food didn't bother me and I always liked the meals and the company that went with them including the ladies who served them. The food wasn't cooked on the premises but was brought in hot containers from some central point.

As I grew older I became aware of how useful and re-assuring a small amount of independent money in your pocket was. With doing odd casual farming work and earning small amounts of money I always had loose change in my pocket. At school meal time I would have the additional choice of going out to buy pies or small confectionary. Although this was only classed as loose change, it was an invaluable tool towards the journey to independence. I think there were few pupils able to take the opportunity. One was my friend John Chalker whose parents were fruit and vegetable wholesalers and lived at "Katymoss" at WaterYeat. He had come to the school from Black-burn with a view to taking the commercial course for later involve-ment in his parents' business. He did go into the family business but later became a car agent at Rainbow Garage in Barrow, selling Lada and Proton cars.

My early years at the secondary school were fairly humdrum. I went along with the crowd without attracting too much attention, operating just below the radar level of detection. If you became good at anything or any subjects you were always expected to perform; if you were at the bottom or last you were ridiculed. It was never my intentions to be either.

I suppose if you were capable of becoming top this wouldn't be much of a problem. but coming top in some subjects, which I did infrequently, always made me uncomfortable because the only way you could go when top was down. Once I reached a certain level I would fight tooth and nail to maintain it. Perhaps it was a case of me just conforming and doing what was basically required and keeping my nose clean. By extending yourself for greater success or achieve-ment you reveal your weaknesses and provide more room for error, and this is the side I erred – perhaps being lazy or unmotivated.

Whilst at school I was involved in other related events taking place in parallel with schooling. Some of these appeared to be insignificant at the time but which later became valuable to me in the overall scope of life.

Sport and athletics were one of my strong points. I represented my house and school at athletics, cross country, football and cricket at junior and senior level. I became house captain of Thirlmere House. In the fourth year I was made a prefect, which was an honour and gave you the chance to support the school staff in the way the school discipline was administered and controlled. This was a good introduction to building relationships and acting as a team member.

I played in the school football team in the Daily Despatch Shield and also had trials for North Lonsdale Boys at Holker Street, the grounds of Barrow Association Football Club. My position at the time was goalkeeper, my reflexes being excellent, but my height went against me and a taller keeper from Dowdales School, Jeff Cornthwaite, got the selection.

On the athletic side I was good at sprinting as well as long distance and won the Urswick sports shield in 1953. It was jointly held with Joyce Atkinson who lived in a bungalow opposite Bolton Manor farm. I think the overall points were tied and we held the shield for six months each.

I had the pleasure of being involved with several sporting brothers at school, playing alongside both the Gifford and the Cumberbatch boys. One of the more memorable was Norman Gifford who was the younger brother of Derek and Tommy and part of a cricketing family. Norman went on to captain Worcestershire Cricket Club and he also played for England on numerous occasions as a slow left arm spin bowler. He eventually became a member of the England selection committee. Joe and John Cumberbatch were the only two coloured boys in the school. Joe was the more robust and stronger athlete, while John was a great sprinter and footballer. Other individuals who had a talent for sport were Derek Porter who played football, and George Hodgson who was a small blonde lad with enormous curly hair who excelled as a sprinter and footballer.

The PE (physical education) teacher lived in my village and he seemed to have a down on me and often made jokes at my expense in front of the class. He once ridiculed me on the sports field when preparing for vaulting over the "horse", suggesting snidely that his wife thought I was lovely especially with regard to the way I was performing. Around the same time when travelling home to Urswick on the bus once, he noticed I had bought a piece of sheet music, "Come back to Sorrento", which I had heard at some time on the radio and thought I would like to play on the piano. He retorted, "What do you want with that? It's a *pub* song." Perhaps he suffered a lack of confidence or perhaps jealousy or both.

Other pupils in my class I remember were Frank Milligan from Newlands who became a pilot; John Brockbank from Birkrigg, a lean, wiry character with ginger hair who excelled at descriptive essay writing and eventually became a chemistry teacher after studying at Leeds University; David Boast from Swarthmoor who, along with several brothers, ended up in various sections of the building trade; Peter Ramsey, a small Ulverston lad whose father was a teacher at Askam; Michael Hyde from Bardsea who's father was the village policeman; Tom Neilson from Swarthmoor who was very tall – over 6 foot at school – and who eventually became a Naval Architect; John Salisbury from Ulverston who was part of a very large family and who became an electrician/electrical engineer; Ronald Whiteway, an Ulverston lad who became a watchmaker; and William Atkinson, a farmer's son from Nibthwaite Grange Farm, Nibthwaite.

The girls that come to mind are Jean Thomson, who became a Domestic science teacher; Sheila Thompson, who was in an unusual position of being the auntie of a boy, Keith Thompson, in the same class; June Sanders; Eileen Jenkinson; Betty Hool, from a farming family at Stewner Park who became a nursing sister and incidently married John Brockbank a fellow classmate; Hazel Hudson; and Ruth Ardron.

Some of my teachers were Peter Thompson – Science; Harry Pilkington – French; Dick Ashburner – Maths; Miss Allison – Biology; Percy Tyson – Geography; Mrs Higham – History; Mr Quilliam – Music; John Cross – Geometrical and Engineering Drawing; and Tim Stockwell – English.

Mr William Bradshaw Walls was the headmaster and Mr Edward Thornton his deputy. Mr Walls was a small, rounded man with a bald head who used a dummy cigarette to try and overcome his smoking habit but who commanded complete authority and respect. The only time I encountered his teaching skill and authority was once when a teacher couldn't take our lesson on a particular subject and, having failed to get a replacement, he stood in at short notice and with the lesson time half way through he immediately took us through a maths exercise on transforming algebraic equations. He took us from the very basics to knowing about transforming equations in a very short time and this brief lesson gave me a complete understanding of the concept. If this had been given with more general information in our maths class I may have not have understood with the same clarity. This was a good example of good teaching; it was given with conviction and clarity.

When pupils first started at the school they were allocated into one of four school houses, which were named after the English lakes – Coniston (yellow), Grasmere (red), Rydal (blue), and Thirlmere (green). Each house had a house master and a boy and girl house captain, and throughout the academic year any achievement in team sports or event that could be quantified went towards house points. This led to a very competitive spirit in the school and it was a proud moment for everyone in the house if you had an individual or a group activity which won points or awards for your house. At the end of each season the captain had to produce an overall report for the school magazine (see Appendix G).

The school's formal, structured system provided me with my core education, but there are many ways of learning in addition to formal lessons and homework. Out-of-school activities offered a different kind of learning through practical and real life situations which brought a fuller concept to education. I had this additional education in the scouts, in my introduction to practical farming, in business activities with my father, and through piano lessons, all which may have made a large contribution to the way I developed and to what I was to do on leaving school and my subsequent family life.

The scouts catered for boys aged 11 to 18, though the optimum age for participants was about 14/15 years of age, and so included boys from the first year to the fourth year at senior school. Mr Grieve, who started the movement in Urswick, asked what type of scouts the community wanted: Air Scouts, Land Scouts or Sea Scouts? It was decided on Sea Scouts. Although not entirely adjacent to the sea, we had the tarn, which is 14 acres (5.7 hectares) in size, and approximately one quarter of mile long, a few hundred yards from the scout meeting place, which was the Sunday school premises adjacent to the church.

The scouts consisted of three patrols of about eight boys each and were named after sea birds: Skua, Artic Tern and Albatross. These patrols were always set tasks to compete against each other. Each had a patrol leader and a seconder, and some kind of pecking order for the more junior scouts. I eventually became patrol leader for the Skua patrol. This gave me some basic skills in leadership and handling people and situations. I always felt comfortable and at ease in this situation.

One of the more formal endeavours of the scouts was the attainment of proficiency badges in various disciplines; for example, astronomy, first aid, fire lighting and cooking. On successful completion of a particular badge it was evidence of a certain level of competency in the relevant topic. The astronomer badge was particularly interesting; not only were we required to understand concepts like the solar system, constellations, star formation and stellar patterns, we had experience first hand because Mr Grieve had a telescope, which at the time would have been considered quite powerful, set up on his vicarage lawn. This offered the experience of the theory and practice all in one. On reflection this gave me an understanding of how the basic structure of atoms and their components are very similar to the universe and its components such as our solar system.

We had to perform part of the cook's badge cooking outdoors; the rest of the tasks were completed in the kitchen of the vicarage. These kitchen tasks were adjudicated by the vicar's wife, who was also the Urswick Guide mistress. I remember that on the day I was to take this badge I had to abandon a driving job on a tractor with John Wood. We were ploughing an area round the perimeter of a stony field near Skelmer Head. We were using the technique known in the farming circles as "ploughing the dyke backs" for getting close to the hedges and walls. John was manipulating a hand plough pulled by the tractor which I was driving. He had to pull the plough off centre by hand and coax it right under the wall. This was quite a physical job because the tractor wheel would not permit you to get right to the hedge or the wall and he had to use physical strength to pull the plough across, as well as walk in the trough of the previous furrows. The field is often very stony near the edges, which would make the plough bounce and shudder in his hands. My appointment for my cooks badge was later that morning and I had to abandon my job so I could go and do it, but the ploughing was near completion.

One week of the year was nationally allocated as "bob-a-job week" by the scouts and cubs. This was to encourage us to perform small tasks for which we were given a "bob" – one shilling or 5p today – and which included gardening, cleaning cars and feeding animals for farmers. All the work done was entered into a special "bob-a-job" card which each scout was given, and all the bobs added up to go towards the scout funds. Many times you received in excess of a shilling; it was a discretionary option whether you kept the extra payment for yourself – so there was an incentive.

Another activity of the scouts were the camping expeditions, especially the annual one in the summer holidays. These included camping in places such as a field near the river Ribble at Grimsargh near Preston, and, on another occasion, in a field adjacent to the river that runs east-to-west at Brampton near Carlisle. One of the more formal campsites was on the Wirral peninsula at a place called Morton, which had an outdoor unheated swimming pool which was one of the coldest pools I had ever experienced. The site was near to the Manchester ship canal. We also visited Liverpool Cathedral and we heard the organ being played at full volume. This was a frightening experience for me and made me feel sickly. We also boarded large passenger ships in the Liverpool docks where we were treated royally because of our sea connection and being in our Sea Scout uniforms. But the most rewarding camps were the ones which involved travelling on the canals around the midlands in two 45-foot canal barges that accommodated about 6 to 8 scouts each and the rest camped on the tow path in tents.

For our annual camp in 1953 we hired the barges from the Canal Cruising Company in Stone, Staffordshire, and the name of the barge I was on the *Mancunian*. There was a 4 mph speed limit restriction to prevent the wake from the boats washing the banks away. There was also the physical and tiring process of using and operating the locks, many of which formed staircases with several locks adjacent to each other. The locks are a device for raising or lowering boats between stretches of water of different levels. This was necessary especially in the Wolverhampton area, where the surrounding area tended to be grey and solemn and much industrialised, but once out of the urban area there was beautiful, placid scenery. Many of the scouts ended up in the water usually due to prankish behaviour or occasionally you had a large pole to direct you away from the banks or other objects but if the scout held on too long or if the pole got stuck in the mud and the boat continued in one direction the scout would be pulled in the other direction and into the water. He might abandon the pole in the canal which would then have to be retrieved.

The camp at Grimsargh near Preston gave us access to the river Ribble and we had the luxury of swimming in the river. At the time my father happened to be in the area with his cattle truck and he called in with his mate, Sammy Hale. Sammy just mentioned to me that my sister had got one up on me in that my dad had bought her a piano. This may seem like an irrelevant comment at the time but it was the beginning of my interest in playing the piano.

During my earlier years in the scouts there was a more senior scout whose name was Raymond Baines, I think. He lived at Stainton and he played the penny whistle and the sound made me curious. He was a few years older than me and the only other thing I could remember about him was that at one camping event he expressed concern about becoming conscripted to the Korean War. This must have been around 1951. But the melodious sound of the penny whistle intrigued me.

The scouts introduced me to the reef, bowline, sheet bend, clove hitch, round turn and two half hitches. All these knots are used to tie, repair or shorten ropes. We were taught splicing, and the construction and operation of a Bosun's Chair Lift which were all demonstrated at camp or on water.

41

One of the events we attended was a jamboree at Preston North End football ground, Deepdale, where our team had to erect a Bosun chair in one corner of the ground and transfer our team from one side to the other.

The scout leader placed a strong emphasis on first-aid training and we were put into teams to tackle various scenarios, from a broken limb right through to serious accidents. We had to display our ability at teamwork in assessing what was required and then administering the first aid. This often required the application of splints and bandages and also to provide a running commentary on what we were doing to the judges to gain points. Our teams were quite successful at various competitions around Lancashire.

We also learnt how to communicate with semaphore, using flags and hand positions. The flags are held in various positions across and away from the body to represent the different letters in the alphabet. This can be used for communication over long distances, so long as the sender and receiver are visible to each other.

Legend or myth has it that the tarn has no bottom, but as part of our scout activities we used a large donated lifeboat to do various exercise on the tarn. We had to propel the boat using muscle power. The boat had three or four oarlocks down each side (port and starboard) and there were usually two scouts to an oar because of their size.

In one of the tarn exercises we had to measure the depth of the tarn at various locations. This was done by throwing overboard a weighted piece of rope that was measured off in fathoms (6 foot) by tying pieces of white rag around it at each fathom. It was gradually lowered over the side until it reached the bottom. Out of all the measurements recorded the maximum depth was six fathoms and that was in the quadrant nearest the church. We discovered that the bottom of the tarn was covered in a reddish sludge which may be due to Clark's Beck which runs into the west side of the tarn from the local, redundant iron ore mines.

We were encouraged to enter the annual Gang Show that was put on in Barrow-in-Furness. All scout groups in the area were invited to audition. Our troop never produced any individual or group contestants that were considered suitable for the occasion. I never had much enthusiasm for it at the time but, on reflection, with more nerve and courage I may have been able to contribute.

One of the more memorable events was the scout's involvement with the soapbox derby. You had to design and develop a pedal car within certain specifications, then build and race it. Our car was named *Ossick Coot* (see Appendix K). There was a separate competition for seniors and juniors. I was selected to represent Urswick Sea Scouts juniors while Maurice Oldcorn raced for the seniors. The team include mechanics James Mossop and Raymond Wilkinson and I was the driver after successful trial runs on a ¼ mile stretch of gently sloping road between Beckside and Skeldonmoor. The official race heats took place on an urban road on the outskirts of Salford and the final along the promenade at Scarborough on the east coast of Yorkshire.

Our pedal car construction was a rather square junky design. The frame was made out of wood and the covering was plywood and sheetmetal, the brake was a plunger which dropped directly onto the ground, and the car had a three-speed gear arrangement operated from the dashboard. The driver sat on the seat in a vertical position with his legs stretched horizontally to the pedals. The design and pedalling arrangements weren't really suited for high power and speed. Many of the other competitors designed their cars as if you were on a bicycle, using foot pressure in a more vertical position, and used fine canvas for lightness, but they were prone to overturning. I didn't manage to get beyond the heat stage because another soapbox car overturned in front of me and balked me which in a quarter mile race left you no time to catch up with the winners; however I did finish at great speed and came fourth or fifth.

On the day of the soapbox derby finals in Scarborough we travelled in the back of a covered truck, along with our soapbox. The 300-mile round journey was completed in a day. I don't think it would be allowed today to travel on the back of a lorry due to Health and Safety and seat-belt requirements.

Among the proficiency badges on offer was the more prestigious "First Class" badge which, you progressed to after receiving your second-class badge. To obtain the first-class badge you had to carry out several activities. One of these was the first-class hike where you had to complete an overnight stay in a tent and cover a certain distance as well as accomplish certain tasks. On completion you had to write a log of the journey.

This hike was usually done in pairs and my partner was James Mossop who was a slim, curly-headed lad who always took a keen interest in sport, and who later became an award-winning journalist with the *Daily Mail*, the *Sunday Express* and the *Sunday Telegraph*.

Our first-class hike took place in July 1951. We received and studied our instructions. The first instruction was to travel to Ulverston and look for the letters O W N W A in a shop's name, enter the shop and seek further instruction by giving the password "Paderewski". We established it was part of the name Downwards Chemist and on giving the password "Paderewski" to the chemist we were given a map with a grid reference of where we had to go and what tasks we had to perform. This was at about 1.30 pm on the Saturday. We also phoned our chief to report any incidents and to say everything was in order.

We arranged transport from Ulverston when we bumped into my father who happened to be in Ulverston at the time and he offered us a lift in his cattle truck. We duly accepted. He dropped us off at Low Field Bridge near Lindal-in-Furness on the road to Barrow. Although this wasn't in the spirit of a hike it was an offer we couldn't refuse. From there we walked up through Marton to the water treatment works and we had to take various samples of water and transfer them to other nearby reservoirs. We also had to sketch all the reservoirs from the top of the fell and then proceed along the road to Horace Farm and Knott Hollow Wood.

Our agent, Paderewski, arrived in his small car with a tent, pegs, mallet and billie cans and further instructions were only given on the password "Nightmares Unlimited". Paderewski's wife was with him and when he was talking to us she pretended to scald her hand on the car radiator. We had to treat her "wound" by making use of bicarbonate of soda.

On Paderewski's advice we went back to Knott Hollow Wood to camp for the night. The farmer at Horace Farm provided us with milk and water. After making a campfire we had supper which consisted of soup and tea. In the morning we made a breakfast of porridge, followed bacon and egg, and afterwards we put more eggs on the fire to hard boil for our dinner.

We took the tent down and packed our kit. The tent was taken to Horace Farm for Paderewski to collect. We then continued on our scheduled journey, walking to Well House through Rake House and following the road into Ulverston, resting at Hollow Mire Road end before finally catching a bus from Ulverston to Pennington lane end and walking the one-and-a-quarter mile to Urswick, arriving there at 12.40 pm on the Sunday. (These details are taken from my first-class hike report which had to be completed as part of the exercise.)

Other After-school Activities

When playing football as an after-school activity I usually had to wait until 6.00 pm for the bus home to Urswick. Some of my other friends from Urswick attended an after-school recorder lesson and I used to wait at the rear of the class for them to finish. Mr Quilliam, the music master, said, "Rather than just sit at the back you might as well join in." He gave me a descant recorder and the tutor book and within the first week I had caught up the class learning the notes played with the left hand fingering (i.e G, A, B, C and D) and by the following week I had surpassed them in completing the notes that required the right hand fingering form (middle C to D, E and F). The fingering for the respective sharps and flats came later. I wasn't proficient at this stage because it takes hours of practice. I must have had a passion to learn because I enjoyed it and progressed pretty quickly.

I remember one related incident which became a bit of an issue. I had to carry my recorder around in my school satchel and one time the recorder fell out and hit the floor. One of the design features of this make of recorder (Schotts descant) is that the bottom holes are split into two separate holes to assist in sharpening or flattening the note. Above these two small holes the (plastic) recorder tapers and then broadens out to accommodate these holes. This is thus a weak area, especially in the plastic ones (the wooden ones don't suffer from this because they are not as brittle), and when dropped usually break at this point. I reported the incident to Mr Quilliam who then referred it to the Deputy Head, Mr Thornton, who asked me how it had happened. I said it dropped out of my satchel and it broke on contact with the concrete floor and I said it was an accident. Mr Thornton was not pleased and said I would have to pay 10 shillings (50p) for a replacement. I told this story to my parents who insisted I shouldn't have to pay. My father said if you have to pay, ask for a receipt. When I requested this from Mr Thornton he became a bit uncomfortable, presumably because he would have to justify his action further up. He then said forget about it, and the matter was dropped. I think asking him for a receipt made him consider whether it was fair and justified, or whether he overreacted. This made me realise that any one who solicits money can have their justification for asking questioned, especially if their action has to become more accountable.

When my father bought the piano for my sister the Smallwood's pianoforte tutor book came with it and I realised that because I had played the recorder I could read the right-hand music (the treble clef). I started taking piano lessons along with my sister. The tutor was Jimmy Dodd who lived two doors away and he charged one and sixpence per hour (7.5p).

He was a shipwright by trade and worked in the shipyard and his skills were also put to good use preserving and maintaining our scout lifeboat which we had on the tarn. He was also the organist for the village and surrounding areas. He was an immaculately dressed man when seen out, but after his wife died he became a bit of a recluse and one day was found dead behind his front door, living in virtual squalor.

This was my first serious introduction to music and I continued my lessons right up to the time I did my GCEs, but with other commitments I found it increasingly difficult to combine the lessons with school work. In the meantime my father had bought me a second-hand 48 bass piano accordion from one of his contacts which I could manage quite well and which I still have and play on occasions when the grandchildren ask for amusement. I also bought a piccolo, a flute and a clarinet from Archie Goodall in the village who was a recognised double base player and band leader. I also managed to obtain a chromatic scale mouth organ. These were eventually sold off as a job lot to Noblet, a second-hand dealer in Barrow. Before I learnt to play any musical instruments I was impressed by the piano playing of Charlie Kunz (1896–1958) who I heard on the valve-operated wireless (radio) at home, listening with my mother in the late forties, early fifties. His style was simple and clear and interpreted the music in a style that was distinctive and endearing.

All these activities were taking place along with my farming activities and helping my father.

It was in late summer when I was about 13 that I wandered into the farmyard of Brian and Ada Wood who had recently started farming on their own at "Midtown". The farm was about 80 acres and was rented from Harold Wood at approximately £6 per acre, which at that time was top of the market rate and was considered a big overhead.

Brian was the third son of John James and Maud Wood who farmed at "Fernleigh", just a few yards along the road, and Ada was the daughter of a farming family who farmed at "Ewedale", a small hill farm above Pennington, off the road from Lowick to Dalton, on the side of Kirkby Moor. I casually asked him if I could help and in no time at all I was feeding calves, pigs, chickens and turkeys.

This became an after-school and weekend activity which expanded, as I got older and stronger, to more strenuous and responsible jobs. The weekend work included mucking out, potato picking, hay making and harvesting. This was to be a life-long friendship and although I was working for Brian he became my first mentor outside the family who I looked to for guidance, and who, by giving me these hard, menial tasks, taught me subconsciously and physically what hard work was. Brian taught me some of the business aspects of farming too, including marketing, pricing, selling, and the art of teamwork and delegation. Being a one-man band, Brian had to depend a lot on casual local labour, although he was also well supported by his wife Ada. The casual labour included people of all ages – from young adolescents to people approaching retirement – and chiefly individuals who were interested in country life like myself and wanted money and a break from their day-to-day non-farming work. Brian had the ability to hone each individual to the task in hand and mobilised a productive, cost-effective team.

My involvement was not just in farming matters. I also provided Brian and Ada with a baby-sitting service for their daughter Marion. This was a duty that included certain privileges like watching their black-and-white television, having access to luxuries such as chocolate biscuits and chocolate log, and also the chance to have free quiet time to do my homework pre-GCE examinations.

With a portfolio of tasks and duties a method of payment had to be established. For baby-sitting I was offered a rate of 2s 6d up to 11.00 pm and 5s afterwards. The rate for the other work was usually by the hour.

When Brian and Ada returned from their night out, Brian never had the correct amount of loose change to pay me for my baby-sitting service. He would say, "book it", and this became the pattern for my payment, not just for baby-sitting but I also logged every aspect of the farming tasks I did as an individual. This did not include the work carried out with a group, when I was paid as part of the group at the end of each day.

I then provided Brian with a comprehensive description of the work carried out. This included number of hours plus baby-sitting duty. I would present the list of various duties and tasks as a type of invoice and Brian would immediately challenge it: "It wasn't *that* many hours," he would say, or query it in other ways, but in the end he saw it was a genuine submission and coughed up. His impulse was to challenge everything – using his own marketing, contracting and tendering skills – and I think it paid dividends for him in his business life. This was my first introduction to the art of bargaining, recording and invoicing.

One of Brian's claims to fame which he always maintains is that he gave me my first earned shilling and he says to everybody he meets in my company to this day that I still have it!

On many occasions Brian would use the phrase, "have you adled it?" when he was giving you money or even providing food on the job. This is a South Cumbria/Furness expression meaning "have you earned it?"

The help I provided for my father was usually on weekends and school holidays when I would travel with him all over Lancashire, Cumberland and Westmorland transporting different types of live-stock, some for local farmers but mainly delivering livestock to abattoirs after they had been sold through the local auctions. On one occasion travelling to Southport from Ulverston with a load of sheep arranged on a decking system that allowed for two levels of sheep in the truck we were pulled over by a police officer on a motor bike at Tarleton, who said, "Sir, I think you were exceeding your speed limit of 20 mph as shown on your speed restriction plate at the rear of your truck". He was a young officer and my father challenged him, saying, "When the truck is full it's important to go just above the speed limit to allow sufficient air flow through the wooden slits in the side of the truck to get a good circulation so the sheep won't suffocate." The young police officer may have had his doubts, but he waved us on.

It was important sometimes that if one of the internal decks collapsed and either killed a sheep or maimed them that is was to be bled right away and you had to get the cooperation of the slaughter men as soon as you arrived. This happened on one occasion when I was with my father when we arrived at a slaughter house in Wigan.

In any business a good control of bookkeeping of the work carried out for invoicing is required and my father had a small, dog-eared notebook in which he logged some rough information and later transferred this to his formal invoicing system. This rough information included the destination, miles travelled, the number and type of animal. In the early years my father had my cousin Leslie Jenkins to do his book work on a Sunday night but as I grew older this was passed on to me and this was my first introduction to bookkeeping.

My father's accounting left a lot to be desired. He sometimes only got around to charging customers – especially local farmers – six months or more after the event and when he came around to doing so he would look in his crumpled handwritten notebook, scratch his head and pluck a figure out of the air.

The deliveries for the Ministry were more formal and better regulated and he received payment on a point system for different animals and the miles travelled. This was the more remunerative part of the business and was consistent and reliable, which is one reason he let the local individual charges to farmers slip, and I would say many got away without payment due to his poor control.

This is an example of how small businesses can fail – lack of control, lack of attention to detail and a complacency about being over-reliant on one major customer.

Just after the war the work for the Ministry was reliable but this finished in the early fifties and more and more farmers were obtaining their own trailers to take their livestock to auction, and business became more selective and competitive.

This was also evident in farming after the war when the more you produced the more you earned, with the added encouragement of the gradual withdrawal of government subsidies, and prices were determined by market forces. Some didn't know how to cope or adjust easily to the new situation. Those that did adapt were the ones who had the business skills to rise to the new challenge.

I have always believed in the enterprise economy perhaps since the nationalisation of road transport in 1947/48. Self-employed owner lorry drivers like my father were not affected and the Road Haulage Association, which my father belonged to, promoted free enterprise. I remember my father had a big map of the United Kingdom on the front over-hang above the roof of the cab of his lorry and smaller ones on the side doors. The map had "Free Enterprise" printed across the top and was supplied by the Road Haulage Association to all members to promote free enterprise rather than nationalisation. At this time I was not quite sure what it meant but as I grew older and developed my own thoughts it became apparent.

My father delivered for local butchers who bought their beasts – calves, sheep etc. – at Ulverston Auction. After the purchase the respective butchers would require the livestock to be delivered to the slaughter house. These deliveries may have amounted to a full load of up to ten cows, or a mixture of sheep, calves and pigs. I used to have to take the invoices along to each individual butchers in Barrow and the market house on a Saturday afternoon. In those days this was the peak time for buying meat in Barrow. Butchers such as Fisher, Redhead, Kerr, Wootton, Banks and Ditchfield come to mind. I used to combine the errand with a visit to the rugby match at Craven Park.

The secret was to hand the invoice over the counter when the shop was full of patrons. The butcher usually settled up immediately: first, they had ready cash in their till and second, they didn't want any embarrassment or delay – an example of understanding the psychology involved when asking for money, so important for cash-flow management.

One of the other services my father provided was to collect items for delivery from Mackereths, the agricultural and seed merchants who were situated above the Market Cross in the market square in Ulverston. These deliveries were to various farming customers on his route. This spared Mackereths from making special deliveries and by going along with him I got a very good insight into the politics and characters of farm kitchens, each having their special menu such as tea, toast and bread and cakes fresh from the ovens. I don't think my father got paid for this delivery services but was given free seed potatoes and other supplies for his own use.

One of the school activities similar to scouting was youth hostling which was undertaken under the school authorities. One particular walk I remember was walking from Keswick to the youth hostel at Red Bank, Grasmere, which was quite an intensive walk via Watendlath and Ashness Bridge, and over the fells to Grasmere in one day. This involved girls and boys and some senior teachers of the school. It provided the experience of walking in the fells of the Lake District and, with your weary legs and other things on my mind, I did not fully appreciate the beauty and pleasure of it. It was not until later, when I was much older, that I was able to digest and absorb that we live in a beautiful area. For my GCE "O" Level English Literature exam we studied in detail the poems of William Wordsworth. At the time to me they were just words ordered into a particular structure, and again it was not until my middle years that I fully valued the meaning and context of Wordsworth's works. Now I nurture and live the words of Wordsworth while out walking, rather than in the confines of a classroom.

A decision had to be made in my fourth year of secondary education, because at the time you could leave school at 15 after the fourth year. The school had introduced a fifth form a few years earlier and it was an option to stay on in the new fifth form to take GCE "O" Level examinations which only a few years earlier was the privilege only of the Grammar School pupils. Pupils in the "A" stream of the fourth year were given the opportunity to carry on into the fifth form to obtain GCE "O" level in a small number of subjects. This decision must have been discussed with my parents and although I was not a high flyer in the "A" form I must have been given the opportunity to benefit from the the extra year. I duly stayed on in the fifth form and as we were relatively few in number we were treated more as individuals than in the previous classroom situation.

The subjects I studied were English Language, English Literature Maths, Biology, Geometrical and Engineering Drawing, and Physics with Chemistry.

I was weak in the two English subjects and it may have been due to the fact that throughout all the previous language lessons I had difficulty in applying what appeared satisfactory in theory in practice for the exams, especially the grammatical structures of sentences with all their relevant clauses. The Literature that was offered was difficult to understand. I enjoy reading but did not enjoy the fictional and the classical work we studied.

I have great respect for spoken English and the value of reading and enjoy scientific, mathematical and technical papers, and publications where topics are tackled in a progressive style, discussing and explaining basic principles and then increasing in complexity. In the English literature classes I always felt I was starting from a different level and if you were not at the accepted level you were continually losing ground –always fire fighting, trying to sort out what had gone before rather than being ahead of the game. Also, its application in life was not clear to me and may have caused obstruction and confusion because it muddled simple logical thinking.

The poetry side of English literature was more enjoyable. Apart from Wordsworth's poetry, the other book we studied was *Caesar and Cleopatra*, a history play by George Bernard Shaw. I got no value from this form of presentation. I never got into the characters and the English dialogue it is written in.

Ironically, I had work published in the school magazine, including a poem called "Winter" (see Appendix G).

My final year at school was the one that counted. It set off as any normal year but the fact the class had taken the option to stay on into the fifth form to take GCE "O" level examinations we could be considered the elite in the school, with only a small percentage of the school pupils in our position. So we had to do our best, although I wasn't conscious of this pressure and worked as directed by the teaching staff with little additional planning myself. I was unaware of the importance of the final outcome and drifted through to the examinations.

The purpose of the extra year was to gain recognised national qualifications and prepare us for work either in a technical or craft environment. Most of the class left school directly after the examinations to seek work. However those who did well were given the opportunity to transfer to the sixth form at the Grammar school to study for "A" levels and beyond.

Education is more than examination results and I attended most of the social functions in and out of school. There were a lot of parties arranged, especially towards the end of term. These sometimes carried on quite late so that we'd miss the last bus to Urswick and had to catch the one to Barrow and get off at Pennington lane end. This left me and others with a one-and-a-quarter mile walk, and we used to make it less boring by "walking a pole and running a pole", measured by the telegraph poles on the roadside.

I left school after the examinations, which were held in May 1955 with the results due out in August. In the meantime I occupied myself by helping my father, attending cattle markets and delivering livestock. My immediate relatives felt I shouldn't be going down that route, but the experience was invaluable for building up intangible and social skills.

I was approaching 17 and the way ahead for me was uncertain. I had obtained the ingredients for my working life and I had, like most people, to make the best and capitalise on the seeds sown. During this period I attended two job interviews, possibly through the careers department in Ulverston. One was at the local Glaxo pharmaceutical factory which was looking for a Laboratory Technician. Glaxo was just developing new pharmaceutical products and they were expanding their factory to increase production of penicillin in their works at the bottom of North Lonsdale Road in Ulverston. The other interview was arranged at Vickers-Armstrong Shipbuilding and Engineering works at Barrow-in-Furness for a position as an Apprentice Metallurgist within their laboratory.

The interview at Glaxo went well but my GCE results were not outstanding and I was competing against more highly qualified individuals from the Grammar school. I remember the girl sitting next to me in the pre-interview room – I think her name was Walmsley – had 8 GCEs from Barrow Grammar School so in the end I was not accepted. However the interview at Vickers was more pragmatic and dealt with broader issues than chemistry

Vickers was a multinational engineering and shipbuilding organisation with numerous works in England and also in Australia and Canada with great product diversity. The one in Barrow included producing submarines, frigates and passenger liners and the engineering works produced a lot of the items that went into these products as well as producing specialised gearing, mining equipment, cement machinery and ship-mounted guns.

I was interviewed by Mr Oldham, Chief Chemist and Metallurgist. He was a formidable character with droopy eyes, a large moustache and a cigarette in the corner of his mouth, and he oozed authority. He was a significant figure in the operation of both sections of the company. He was accompanied by his assistant George Williams who was a smart, dapper, academic type of person who later taught me chemical metallurgy at night school. His sense of humour was unique and partly sarcastic. He had limited social skills but his knowledge of chemistry and metallurgy couldn't be questioned. In the interview Mr Oldham asked whether I helped with the repair and maintenance of my father's cattle truck. I said yes and gave a brief outline of what I did. He said part of the work I would be involved in was climbing to the top of ships with a radioactive isotope to take radiographs. This was difficult to comprehend then but it seemed something I could manage.

One of the principles Mr Oldham instilled later in me and every other member of the laboratory staff was that when visiting other works or attending seminars or conferences the job was not complete until a report had been written and he had a principle of not signing off any expenses incurred without a report attached or in place.

The laboratory report covered where you had been and for what purpose, who you had met and any outcome. This was always filed as a laboratory report and was available for reference for anybody interested in the information or for any other member of staff who may be making a return visit. This discipline has remained with me.

There must have been something about me to be considered suitable for the apprenticeship as there was a strict approach of taking on apprentices for the company, especially in a staff position. An apprenticeship was offered and subsequently I had to sign indentures to the terms and conditions which were witnessed by my father and representatives of the employment department (see Appendix I).

This was not classed as a general trade or craft apprenticeship but a staff technical apprenticeship and gave me full staff status from the time I joined the company. This had a higher status than the works apprentice; the hours of work were less – 38 hours, 20 minutes as opposed to 44 hours – with sick pay and additional holiday entitlement too.

One of the factors at the time that wasn't apparent was the rules and conditions of the staff pension scheme. These rules included the indication that your years of service started from the day you started on the staff not from the time you joined the pension scheme, which you were not permitted to do until aged 21. These extra five years of service without contribution was a big perk and may not apply today.

The method of on-and-off the job training was entirely suited to the job in hand. One of the requirement of the general trade apprenticeships was to spend the first few weeks in what was called Hunters

Yard Apprentice Training School, where you were taught the basics of using tools and shaping metals in engineering. For my type of technical apprenticeship this did not apply and I became involved with the everyday work of the laboratory and the x-ray department.

This may give the impression that I had direction to my way ahead. This was far from the truth. I was in a state of limbo, getting up each day to the events that were coming my way, without much ambition and foresight. But I always felt I would do all right whatever direction my life might take.

CHAPTER THREE

1956–1962
Aged 17–23 Years
Apprenticeship

"No wonder Hadrian built a wall"

On Monday 17th October 1955 I started as an apprentice metallurgist in the laboratory at Vickers Armstrong Engineering Works at Barrow-in-Furness, which employed about 3,000 people, and the associated shipbuilding works employed a further 4,000. Both works were within the same boundaries and only divided by the road. The laboratory provided a metallurgical service to both works.

My starting date was not the same as the annual intake of apprentices because other trade and technical apprentices commenced in September. I don't know how this came about but it may have had something to do with staffing levels and a position becoming vacant.

The hours of work were from 8.40 am to 5.30 pm with an hour and ten minutes for lunch, from Monday to Friday. I had a privileged finishing time of 5.18 pm which was the works employees finishing time. This was to allow me to catch the service bus which left outside the works in Michaelson Road for my journey home through other villages to Urswick. The bus was usually a red double-decker bus run by Ribble Bus Company and it was always full. The bus would pick us up at about 8.10 am outside the Derby Arms in Urswick. If I had to work unsociable hours I would cycle to work which took about forty minutes. My route went up Horse Close and Stone Dike Lane via Mascelles, joined the main Ulverston to Barrow A590 at Crooklands, and then continued on to Barrow down Abbey Road. The bus journey into Barrow at 8.10 am catered specifically for the staff employees because the works employees started at 7.30 am and caught a much earlier bus. The return journey home catered for everybody and the discussions and debates on the bus took on a wider and social context and added interest to the ride.

I enjoyed the camaraderie of the journey. There was a mixture of passengers; some worked in the offices and young ones like myself were trainees and just starting their working lives. These included Audrey Goodall and her friend from Ulverston, Eileen Preston, and Doreen Marshall who was picked up at Stank Road end. Audrey and Eileen worked in the tracing office under a very strict boss, Miss Ethel Hancock, and any conversation usually included talk of how Ethel was treating them or their latest confrontation with her.

There was a clear distinction between the contractual conditions of work employees and staff employees. The works people were paid by the hour and worked a basic week of 44 hours, and the staff were paid by the week and worked 38 hours 20 minutes. The more senior staff were paid monthly, and this formed a three-tiered pecking order. There was a greater allocation of holiday entitlement for the staff; the works employees were entitled to 10 days annual leave in addition to the statutory ones whilst the staff employees were entitled to 15. This inequality of employment hours and holiday entitlement was a big factor in those days which today has been abolished with all workers having the same hours and other more uniform conditions of employment.

I started work with a completely open mind with no preconceived ideas or direction. I just went where the wind blew me, but I always admired how a company employing so many people and manufacturing such a diverse range of products of huge complexity, size and integrity produced such world-class shipbuilding, engineering and armament products. Just how did they manage it?

One of the reasons was the shipbuilding and engineering works employed a vast variety of skills, professional expertise and characters. The complex organisation had the capability of designing, manufacturing, testing and solving problems of diverse engineering products and the key was how it was all brought together. This must have been a result of effective management and direction, combined with a sense of purpose from the employees.

My apprenticeship involved working alongside journeymen who

had just completed their apprenticeship and trained technicians. The five-year training programme included attending day release and night school. There was no locally recognised national training programme in metallurgy and non-destructive testing mainly due to low demand and because it was neither considered a craft or a trade apprenticeship which had their own national guidelines and qualifications including City and Guilds, the Ordinary National Certificate (ONC) and the Higher National Certificate (HNC). It was then up to the company to produce its own in-house training programme that would cover what they wanted. Day release was provided to attend relevant courses which were designed and approved of by the training department and the laboratory to suit the nature and type of work the company was involved in.

On reflection this was a pioneering stage in the training of Non-Destructive Testing (NDT) personnel. This method of testing materials and products is applied without destroying or altering their properties. This was done by using radiography and ultrasound, which were used to detect sub-surface imperfections, whilst penetrant inspection and magnetic particle inspection was used to detect surface imperfections. All of these disciplines were to play a major factor in quality assurance programmes that were being developed for industry worldwide. This training was well focussed and directed. It produced the skills and knowledge that was required to test the company's products without overtraining or undertraining personnel. I think many companies would get value if they tailor-made their training to suit their own requirements while still including the core skills to be competent at the job.

The day release involved attending the local technical school, first in Abbey Road and then at the new premises in Howard Street, Barrow-in-Furness.

As part of my training programme I studied GCE "A" levels in Physics, Chemistry and Maths and the evening class covered metallurgy, including both physical and chemical analysis aspects. Along with this we were expected to take up approvals (qualifications) in Non-Destructive Testing. One of these involved attending the one-month course on industrial radiography at the Kodak School of

Industrial Radiography at its factory at Harrow-on-the-Hill just north of London. On successfully passing this course you were permitted to view and accept radiographs against the respective contractual standards. This course was approved by Lloyds Register of Shipping for any of their surveillance work which other organisations accepted, including the Ministry of Defence. The location of the school meant I had to stay in Harrow-on-the-Hill for the duration of the four weeks.

Harrow was handy for the rail link to London with the train taking about 30 minutes. The Kodak factory facilities included the School of Industrial Radiography, which had good social clubs and I was free to attend.

I stayed in digs about 15 minutes walk from the Kodak factory school. The couple who I stayed with had a five-year-old son and the father worked at the Kodak factory. Although I arrived late on a Sunday evening because of the laborious train journey all the way to Euston station and then a change to the tube which brought me back out of London to Harrow, they made me very welcome.

The social options included going to local dance halls. On one occasion while I was waiting outside one dance hall a large Rolls Royce pulled up with the registration MB1 and the person who got out, wearing dark sunglasses, was Max Bygraves the popular singer and entertainer of the day. All the young girls rushed to him and he gently shoved them away, remarking, "get back to your husbands or boyfriends". One weekend I made a visit to London Airport where I enjoyed watching large planes landing and taking off. This must have been the small version of Heathrow today.

At the Kodak school I was influenced by Dr Mullins, head of the school, and his assistant John Grimwade, both very distinguished people in the industrial radiography scene and pioneers in its development. I shall always be grateful for what they and Wilf Cotton, my manager at Vickers, did for me in my early days of industrial radiography.

Non-Destructive Testing was a relatively new discipline carried out by laboratory staff. The more run-of-the-mill work included macro and micro examination of metals, heat treatment and pyrometer control, tensile strength and surface hardness testing and the investigation following metallurgical failures. All these aspects were covered as part of our apprenticeship. There was another section of the laboratory that carried out chemical analysis and associated disciplines. As an apprentice we were allocated a short time in these sections to be made aware of what each part of the laboratory did and how it served the company.

I was taken on at the time when there were only about five people involved with NDT out of a laboratory staff of about 30.

During my apprenticeship, due to the growing contractual requirements of the nuclear submarine build at Barrow, demand for NDT expanded as NDT inspection became mandatory to meet the ever-increasing requirement of quality assurance that the new equipment and build specifications imposed.

There developed a need to train additional people to assist in this inspection. The company took on people as NDT assistants who helped with aspects of radiography, surface flaw detection and ultrasonic testing, depending on what was needed and what skills they brought to the job. In the early days it was accepted that surface flaw detection was the easier discipline to be trained in, followed by radiography and then ultrasound. These people were always under the supervision or guidance of qualified technicians.

By the time I completed my apprenticeship there were at least 50 people involved in NDT. This was mainly due to the requirements for building the first British nuclear submarine, *Dreadnought*. Many of its materials and structures required NDT examination. The sort of testing done was based on the standards established by the American nuclear submarine programme, as that country had built several submarines previously and had established standards.

With the American involvement in the early stages of the development and start of the production of *Dreadnought* I had the pleasure of meeting Admiral Rickover who was known as the "Father" of the US nuclear navy and was one of the most prominent people involved in establishing the Quality and Assurance standards to meet the demands of the nuclear submarine programme. He came to visit Vickers at Barrow to meet Len Redshaw (later Sir Leonard Redshaw), the leader of the Vickers build for the British nuclear submarines, and as part of his visit he came into our department where we were inspecting the welds of a main component of the nuclear reactor cooling system. The facilities had to be clinically clean and he remarked that we were overdoing it. He was a small man in a black raincoat and a trilby hat.

My work involved the radiography of engineering and shipbuilding structures and components. Radiography involved the use of an electrical x-ray machine (x-rays) or a radioactive isotope (gamma rays) which emitted the type of radiation that was suitable for penetrating metal in a reasonable time and which was recorded as images on film. This film (the radiograph) was tangible and could be assessed after the event or at some time in the future. When outside inspection authorities came to view the radiographs the quality of the radiograph and how it was presented provided them with confidence not only about what we did but also about the general quality and assurance of the company's product.

Radiography had one advantage over other methods of NDT in that the resultant image was produced on film (called a radiograph, not an x-ray as is often assumed) which could be viewed and considered by other relevant personnel at a later date. Most of the other inspections meant viewing in real time as the inspection took place. Magnetic and penetrant methods were used to detect surface breaking imperfections. At the time ultrasound methods of examination were in their infancy. This method involved passing high frequency sound into the material and assessing any faults from the received reflected signals from imperfections or if the sound was attenuated when passing through the metal. All the transmitted and received sound impulses were portrayed on an oscilloscope and it required specialised skills to interpret these signals. Over the years all these methods became more user-friendly, with approved procedures and trained personnel making them easier to apply. Radiography was the most capital intensive, with stringent safety controls and regulations due to the radiation being used.

Although NDT is classed as technical work, to apply this discipline to the company products meant a lot of climbing, crawling and physical effort to get equipment into position, no more so than in the bottom of a nuclear submarine reactor room amongst the jungle of pipes which were in place to carry coolant to and from the reactor, and also in many boiler compartments with narrow access between bundles of pipes, as well as right up to the very top of the ship's structures using intricate staging and scaffolding.

At that time (1955) the maximum amount of radiation we were permitted to receive was stipulated and the radation we received was recorded on personal dosimeters which we wore on our clothing. One of these was a pencil-shaped ionisation chamber which, as it received radiation, discharged itself in proportion to the radiation received. This was calibrated through an eyepiece through which we could view the amount of radiation received. The meters were read officially each week and returned to zero and recharged for use the following week; an advantage of this was that it could be read immediately. The other method of measuring the radiation received was the use of a film badge which was a piece of film about 30mm square housed in a plastic holder which was made up of small filters and which was clipped to our clothing. Each month the film was sent for processing by the National Radiation Protection Board. The amount of radiation received was established and the filters also indicated which type of radiation – beta, gamma or x-rays – the wearer had been exposed to.

This amount of radiation was the official record and would eventually tell you of your lifetime dose, not including any medical x-rays or natural radiation you received whilst not at work. By the time of my retirement in March 1994 I had received a lifetime dose of 310.1 millisieverts. The recommended lifetime maximum occupational limit is 400 millisieverts.

The radiation for industrial radiography came from two different emitters of radiation. One was from x-ray machines which were worked electrically and could be switched off when no radiation was emitted. The second, however, was radioactive isotopes that are continually emitting radiation, and the radiation source was housed and sealed in a lead/heavy metal container referred to as the "bomb". Part of these sealed "bombs" had a door that could be opened to allow a pencil beam or cone of radiation out. Even when these doors were closed a small amount of radiation was present. There was no apparent danger so long as you were not handling it or near it 24 hours a day. The radioactive isotopes were housed in sealed pellets usually 1x1 mm or 2x2 mm and up to 6x6 mm in size. The ones used were Iridium 192, Caesium 137 and Cobalt 60, all of which had their different specific wavelength and hence penetrating capabilities and also had individual rates of decay over time known as the half life.

Once the radioactivity had reduced to an impractical level it was my duty to send them to Harwell Atomic Facilities in Oxfordshire for reactivating. With up to 30 of these isotopes in use it was important they were controlled and changed at the optimum time. This was arranged through Vickers' own transport and usually involved six or seven isotopes at a time. The vehicle that was used for transport had to carry the correct signage and report to a local police station if it involved an overnight stay with them on board.

The fact we were dealing with ionising radiation meant we required periodic medicals and in the early years we had to undergo a blood check every three months. It was also determined that the younger you were the greater the potential for radiation damage and hence if under 18 years of age you were restricted to the numbers of hours overtime you were allowed to work which was about six hours over the basic working week. This was applicable to me for the first two years.

With the department expanding rapidly a structure of management, supervision and an in-house training scheme had to be established. The people taken on for this work came from different walks of life including tradesman from within the company as well as others from outside the company were given an opportunity to apply. With being young and on a technical training scheme I became involved in passing information onto the new recruits and also taking on responsibilities.

When I started my apprenticeship there was another apprentice who had started in the September under the same employment conditions as me. His name was Brian Lennon. Brian and I worked together and shared similar experiences in the way we were treated and trained. Brian had different characteristics to myself and turned out to be a natural leader, always seeing the bigger picture and always looking for the opportunity to move on. I was more technical and less ambitious and concentrated more on the work in hand.

Brian was to become influential in my life in the fact that he encouraged me to follow him in taking supervisory and management courses which were being introduced at the local college.

One of my first, basic, mundane non-technical duties, along with Brian, was to take the section's staff white overalls for laundering and collect clean ones on a Monday morning. These free issue overalls were also another perk at the time as the works employees had to provide their own and were responsible for their laundering and replacement.

The overall collection place was adjacent to the pay office where we collected our wages every Thursday. The basic first year net pay was £2 9s 1d (£2.50).

I spent most of my apprenticeship in the x-ray department which was situated away from the laboratory under the management of Wilf Cotton and his deputy Ken Norman and along with their assistant Tom Smith, who all brought to the department different practical skills and innovations and ways of adapting materials into jigs and fixtures. This cave-like department was known as the "Crypt" because it was housed underground under the road between the armament drawing office and the engine shop. This facility was ideal for radiography because it had self-shielding walls for the radiation. Access to it was limited, but for the delivery of large items it could be accessed through two large lead-lined doors from the pit in the engine shop were they used to test large marine engines.

There was also a satellite department based in the shipyard under Walter Sansom and his assistant Les Ashurst. All these people had a big influence on me, especially Wilf Cotton who had worked with x-rays at Manchester University and obtained a master of science degree and had the technical and academic capabilities of working things out from basic principles. Not only was he an asset and tutor to the department and to those who worked under him but he was one of the most underestimated men in the whole company.

Walter's training was as a metallurgical chemist in the laboratory and he had been a prisoner of war. He used very descriptive verbal and written language, and was one of those chaps who are very interesting for a short period but if you had prolonged, compulsory times with him he could be rather annoying and unpredictable.

It became obvious when I first met Walter and observed his mannerisms that he was the brother of Leslie Sansom, the works photographer who took our photographs in the late forties when playing in Urswick and on Bardsea beach when he visited his mother-in-law at Bank End. His mannerisms were exactly the same and he always tried to emulate his brother's photographic and journalism skills.

I admired Ken's application of vocabulary and his journalistic approach to writing reports. Les, on the other hand, was just a few years older than me and had come to the job after being a dental technician in the army. Les was very tall and thin and wore a flat cap and smoked full-strength Capstan cigarettes. One of his strong characteristics in my mind was his politeness and friendly approach.

One feature that Wilf, Ken and Walter all had in common was their love and interest in photography. The fact our work involved processing x-ray film made it partly compatible with photography. These were the people who introduced me to photography and it wasn't long before I was producing good work and taking small orders for children and group photographs. I had established darkroom facilities in my parent's house and later in my own house. I made use of a 3¼ x 2¼ inch square enlarger which Tom Smith and I knocked up from second-hand material. Tom was a very practical man.

I soon realised that it could be false economy photographing children with just one uncle and aunt and I always considered the potential market of the ones who had unlimited relations. In 1960 I entered a photographic competition through the *Scots Magazine* a magazine produced in Scotland with a big UK and worldwide circulation.

The photograph was of a Scottish piper playing his bagpipes with his daughter or granddaughter by his side in Glencoe. The entry won second prize in the black-and-white section and I won £5. The winner receiving £25. This was not the last I heard of it. After I got my cheque and acknowledgement I then got further correspondence through the editor from a disgruntled Scotsman from Aberfeldy saying this photograph should never have been published and it was a disgrace to the Scottish national dress and if Mr Elleray wants to photograph Scotland he should come up and photograph the St Andrews Pipe Band.

I replied through the editor and said, "No wonder Hadrian built a wall", and I implied I got out of Scotland what I wanted: £5.

Not only that, there was reference to it in the next month's magazine, when it was reprinted in a thumbnail size alongside a letter from another reader who said it should have been in a "guess-who" competition, not a photographic competition. The editor replied and said the photograph was judged on purely photographic merit and not the subject matter.

The first camera I bought was a 3¼ x 2¼ Voiglander Bessa with a viewfinder and bellows, and this was followed by a second-hand twin lens Rolliflex Automat 1938 which cost £40 in 1960 and I have it still to this day but never use it. Wilf, Ken, Tom and others in the department were by then into colour transparencies. I stuck with black-and-white for a long time.

During my apprenticeship I was living at home and my father was still self-employed. He was getting to an age where his work was becoming physically demanding for him. Business was also dropping off and becoming more competitive. The idea of me taking the business over was discussed but only in general terms, and it was agreed I would be better off doing what I was doing. I was never really interested and took the lead from my experienced father rather than my own inexperienced view of the situation. There were other factors which had to be taken into consideration. I was not eligible to drive and any increase in tonnage from the current 3-ton vehicle would mean I would have to wait until 21 years of age to drive it. I think the age difference between me and my father was a big deciding factor. I was too young and he was too old to create the synergy to become a successful business.

I learnt to drive with my father's tuition in the small Morris van he had. When I failed my test my father was surprised I had failed and asked the examiner why. The examiner said there was nothing wrong with my driving but I failed on the theory questions on the Highway Code. One of the questions I remember was "What is the difference between a halt sign and a slow sign?" And I said, "One says halt, the other says slow." That wasn't the answer they were looking for. It was the difference in shape, I think: one was square and the other round. This may have been due to my father being a driver and not a theory man. Today you are expected to learn from an authorised driving instructor.

Although I did pass my driving test when I was eighteen after the second attempt, another aspect that came into play was that at eighteen I would be due for two years national service which was mandatory and which would take me away from the business for that period, too prolonged a break to keep the business viable. When I became eligible for national service at the end of my five-year apprenticeship it had come to an end I was no longer required to serve. I received notification in October 1960.

The decision not to get involved with the business was one I have never regretted.

I still enjoyed being involved in village life, and this included my duty as a server at the church. I was on a rota helping the vicar with the blessing and serving the communion wine.

One Christmas day service, held at 7.00 am, I was on duty and I embarrassed myself a little. After partying the night before I attended the church on an empty stomach. The wine chalice was full to the brim, and as servers we were given the first swallow and because it was so full I supped quite a large amount it hit the bottom of my stomach and I began to feel unwell. Reclining back to my kneeling position at the side of the alter as the congregation was forming a line along the alter rail I became dizzy and fell over backwards. The next thing I knew I was been carried down the isle, in the reverse order of a funeral. They took me to the back of the church and I was soon perfectly fine. One of the people who helped me was Sheila Stables from Huntide farm who was a nurse.

I returned home at about 8.00 am and tucked myself into bed without my parents being any the wiser. The only problem was neighbours and friends came round to ask how Geoffrey was and my mother asked why, and they said he fainted in church this morning. I was woken to give an explanation.

Although I attended church on a regular basis I had difficulty in comprehending the sermons and the preaching. The vicar was rather high church and I was lost by his imaginative and rhetorical style. It seemed insincere at times, but to be a good story. I enjoyed the congregation style of singing hymns as well as the organ music. I was in my early to middle teens I became aware of an intimidating and pontificating approach at times. From a young age I was under the impression that the creation of the world as described in the Bible and the birth of Jesus all supposedly happened in a relatively short period of time. When you become aware that it is only 2,000 years since Jesus was preaching you realise that Christianity is relatively new. Then there follows the debate: What *is* time? Is it as we visualise a chronological happening of events, or some figment of our imagination that we can't comprehend. At the moment we are having the thought about time, time has gone and the future hasn't arrived! What was not precise in biblical teaching was the concept of time. An event or epoch is described as "a long time ago", or this age and that age, without the dates and relationship in time being quantified. This is difficult to comprehend when you are at school.

The teaching of Christianity has good intentions and is an excellent moral and theoretical guide to how life should be lived. I felt there could be other equally legitimate principles on the way we should behave and conduct our affairs. For example, I feel that religious preaching is not unlike the use made of fairy stories – Father Christmas and the tooth fairy. Over the last 2,000 years people have preached to subsequent generations, and being passed down in that way the teachings become truths, and it may be one big illusion, but nevertheless the faith and deliverance is a paradigm that shouldn't be underestimated or devalued. Religion shouldn't stop one thinking for oneself, but you should have an open mind and try to act responsibly within your constraints and feel comfortable with who you are.

In my spare time I remained active with farm work and on occasions Brian Wood asked me if I would do the milking for him while he, Ada and Marion went on holiday for a few days.

This I did and the responsibility meant getting up at 6.00 am each morning, collecting the dozen or so cows from the field up the road from our house and taking them to the shippon at Midtown farm for milking. Each cow had its allocation of feed and the milk was collected in aluminium milking containers each of which had a pulsator attached to it to create the vacuum to draw the milk from the cow. The milk was then carried by hand and emptied into a milk holder on top of a vertical cooler down which it ran, cooled by the running water flowing through inside. It then entered a sieve which was on top of a 12-gallon milk churn/kit. At the end of each session there were usually three to four full churns which had to be on the milk stand by 8.30 am for collection the following morning by the milk lorry. The churns were dragged horizontally from the horizontal slab of the milk stand across onto the flat of the lorry. Replacement empty churns would be left and on occasions when in summer the milk had remained on the stand in the summer heat it would turn sour before it got to the dairy. These would also be returned and it wasn't a very pleasant job first of all discovering the ones that had been returned, and secondly, dispensing with the smelly curdled contents, conscious of the lost value of the wasted milk.

After each milking session the cows had to be returned to their grazing field which was situated on the edge of the village residential area. With another four or five farmers doing the same there was the occasional almighty mix up usually at the open space outside the Derby Arms pub and Bankfield. It took some sorting out whose cows were whose but the secret to avoid this was timing so that all the cows were not in the road at the same time.

My work was overseen by Brian's father, John James Wood, a farmer himself who lived a few yards away from the farm. His style of overseeing was not intrusive. I could always tell his presence by the smell of his pipe tobacco which floated in the air preceding him. He would see the milk churns on the stand at the bottom of the yard and walk up and ask me some simple questions such as "How is the agricultural worker?" and I would say, "Fine, Mr Wood." But while he asked the question he was scanning the cattle and the yard. And then he would walk away. A very good way of overseeing. He saw enough to be reassured things were satisfactory. The milking procedure was repeated in the late afternoon. The milk stayed in the dairy to be combined with the following morning's milk. After each milking session the dairy and the equipment had to be scrupulously washed and the shippon mucked out.

During the day I had a few other duties to perform including dealing with the odd irate customer who had been supplied with some not so good potatoes.

Brian had started to establish a potato marketing service to local shops from his own grown potatoes. He however wanted to expand this further and to make it a substantial part of his farming life. To establish and test the market we would set off to Barrow in a van and seek out potential customers amongst the shopkeepers. We would take it in turns to approach the different shops. Some would say definitely not, while others were prepared to sample them and if our luck was in we made a sale and obtained repeat orders.

To establish the business Brian had to go before the Potato Marketing Board to obtain a wholesaler's licence to do this work. They had to take into consideration the existing wholesalers in the area and whether there be enough demand. One of the questions they asked him was would he be able to guarantee the supply of potatoes to meet his customer requirements, and he said he had three other brothers in the farming business and other farming contacts, and he duly got the licence.

This exercise in cold selling to shops intrigued me and helped me with how to approach, negotiate and deal with people.

My social life was integrated with my working life and associated activities which also included at least two nights of overtime and two evenings at night school. I was a regular visitor to the dances in

Ulverston's Coronation Hall, hunt balls and village dances in the countryside as well as the odd night at the Rink and Palace dance halls in Barrow.

It was at the New Year's Eve dance at the Coronation Hall in Ulverston in 1955/56 that I met my wife-to-be, Doreen. I was with a crowd of my mates and she was sat at the left-hand side halfway down along with her friends and elder sister Marjorie.

Doreen was part of a farming family who farmed at Beckside farm, Colton, in the Colton/Oxen Park valley between Greenodd and Satterthwaite. She was the fourth child of Robert and Eleanor Phillipson having two elder sisters and a brother as well as a much younger sister. Doreen left school at 15 to help her mother with her domestic duties on the farm, which were quite demanding, having to cater for their family and agricultural workers.

Although similar to what I had been used to in Urswick, the type of farming her family did was different in the way it was approached. At the Urswick farm, which was relatively small, animals were bought in and fattened up for sale rather than reared from scratch, whilst the Colton farm was much larger and included a mixture of good land, fell and woodland. Doreen's father, and subsequently her brother, farmed this land to produce good quality stock, grain and vegetables as well as clearing a lot of the fell land into more productive grazing land. Doreen's father's work ethic and attention to detail and quality was second to none.

"Old Bob", as he was known, was a hard taskmaster during the day, progressing the work in hand as hard as possible. He was virtually unapproachable, speaking only to comment on work or instruct how he wanted things doing.

At 6.00 pm when the day's work was over he was a different man, and he completely shut off from work until the following morning. With the responsibilities he had with a large family and farm to run this was an attribute which I admired. On one occasion I remember he saw me coming across the fields on the tractor and challenged me, saying I should have come around by the road. "I can't afford for you to come over grass at eight pound a yacker [an acre]", he said. However, after 6.00 pm if I asked him for the use of his car so that

Doreen and I could go out there was no question, and he would also provide funding for the petrol.

My courting days introduced me to a different approach to farming and all the supplementary Lakeland countryside activities such as hunting and poaching. I was familiar with the North Lonsdale fox hounds because my father used to transport them about in their designated area known as North Lonsdale and I became acquainted with Coniston fox hounds because Doreen's relations were involved. There was a beck running through the farm where a lot of salmon bred and many a night I joined poaching sessions with the farm workers and Walter, Doreen's brother. Alternatively we would go out shooting hares by using Walter's pick-up for transport across the fields, equipped with good headlights and supplemented with others mounted on the pick-up. Once the hares were in beam they were as good as shot. At Christmas time we would collect holly from out of the wood and have a stand at Barrow market so Walter could make some spare cash.

In the early courtships days Doreen and I only used to meet up about once a week on a Saturday night to attend the Roxy picture house in Ulverston. First we would have coffee or ice drinks in *Deganis's* coffee shop in Market Street, along with other young couples out for the evening. My method of transport at the time was by bus but Doreen had the luxury of been chauffeured about by her brother Walter in a Morris Oxford car, Reg. LS 5208, and later perhaps in the pick-up. Eventually I had a moped, a 50cc single cylinder NSU Quickly which I used to get from Urswick to Colton. Later I used my parent's Morris car. The car cost £40 from Dan Lowther in Ulverston and one foggy night I left Beckside and turned right at the white gate and followed the road to the top at Springfield where the road forks to the right going down into Spark Bridge. The junction is divided by a grass patch with a large boulder on it and somehow in the fog I must have wandered and I ran high and dry onto it. I had to get Doreen's brother Walter out of bed to take me home to Urswick. The car was a right-off due to a broken chassis.

My spare time at weekends and during holidays would be spent helping out at both the farms in Urswick and Colton, and formed part of my getting to know Doreen. From this you may think our courtship was pragmatic and unemotional but it was carried out in a loving and caring way. I must admit I wasn't the most romantic of characters but more consistent, predictable and genuine. I know self praise is no recommendation but I must have been a good catch.

Doreen and I shared the same core values of working together and farming and country life. Doreen's special qualities were her ability to provide the home comforts and her tenacity to work hard. She was also a leader in fashion of things outside the agricultural norm. What I did notice was her ability to think beyond the obvious. This was apparent one time when we were driving up a narrow road in the Lake District and there was a lady standing on the right-hand side of the road. I had hardly noticed her but Doreen said there is a bus coming and a few minutes later we met a bus head on but with little space to pass. I saw her simply as a lady; she saw her as a lady expecting a bus. This happens today; when viewing television programmes she is not thinking about the main theme but is analysing and criticising the colour of three-piece suits or the inappropriate dress of men such as brown shoes with a dark suit or the assortment of multicoloured sock combinations men wear. These are observations of an alert and questioning mind.

Annual holidays were usually in the last week in July and first week in August and were known as the Vicker's shut down. In two consecutive years (1956 and 1957) I went with some of my mates to Butlin's holiday camps at Fily on the east coast of Yorkshire. These friends included John Chalker who worked for his parents and brothers in the Fruit and Vegetable Wholesale business, Anthony Tracy (Tant) a lad from the village, Tom Jackson and Rolly Edmondson, both farmer's sons who worked on the respective farms of Bolton Manor, Little Urswick and Rolly at Broughton Beck just to the north of Ulverston.

This was when this type of holiday – "fully packaged", including entertainment and accommodation – was taking off. Young people from all over descended on the various Butlin's Holiday camps around the country. It was the first opportunity for many to take two weeks holiday and enjoy themselves with likeminded people. We travelled by train via Carnforth, Hellifield and Leeds to the Yorkshire coast. The accommodation was a chalet type arrangement with room sharing. We were woken at 7.00 am each morning by the tannoy system wishing a good morning to every camper and announcing the highlights of the day's events. I joined in many: boxing, running and talent competitions – playing the penny whistle – and the evening entertainment and dances.

Doreen and I enjoyed holidays in Scotland when we had the use of her brother's Austin A55 pick-up vehicle to travel and explore Scotland, staying at B&Bs and public houses.

In 1957 my father decided to sell his business. He was approached by John Stables, a local farmer, who was aware that he was ready for packing up. He farmed in Little Urswick and as part of his farming activity he wanted to bring an additional service for his business and to incorporate his son-in-law, Eric Phizacklea, and employee, Horace Scott, who would drive the truck. The business itself was a service business and there were no assets involved only the good will of the business and the second-hand value of the cattle truck. What was of value was the licence that went with it.

The licence, an "A", allowed you to transport anything anywhere in the country and was not easily obtainable. Other types of licence included "B" and "C", "B" allowing you to transport within a certain radius of your business and the "C" licence used by farmers to transport their own stock. The sale value of the business was £700 and I would say 75 per cent of that was for the licence.

A few months following the sale my father took up employment as a mechanic in a company in Barrow and then with Hoggarth's Agricultural Engineers at Ulverston, a big distribution and repair company for farm machinery and parts under the managership of Mr Cope. He was employed as a storeman and maintained this position full time and then part time into his early seventies.

Towards the end of my apprenticeship things in my personal life were beginning to evolve and it became clear for Doreen and I that we wanted to get married. I had to ask Old Bob, her father, for his permission. All he said was "Aye. But thou's tecking a lot on". I didn't know whether this was complimentary to Doreen or not, but she had a lot of good qualities and I was prepared to take a chance.

Decisions had to be made on such issues as where to live and where to access funding for the forthcoming commitment.

I was quite thrifty and had a propensity to save but Doreen was more limited from having worked at home. She wasn't afforded a wage but was giving a small remuneration at the end of each week – 10 shillings (or 50p today) – to cover incidentals and if she required the additional luxuries of a new dress or a pair of shoes she had to go cap-in-hand to Old Bob, who always offered a good reason why she didn't need them, but with Doreen's persuasion she usually managed something even if it had to be a compromise. She was well provided for at home, a type of payment in kind in return for her being a valuable asset in the running of the farm.

Just prior to our marriage as part of my work I was sent to the Admiralty Research and Testing Establishment (ARTE) at Dounreay on the northern tip of Scotland for several weeks, where the future nuclear reactors and propulsions systems for submarines were being developed, installed and tested. The company supplying the NDT services at the time had run into difficulties with the huge amount of inspection to be done and asked for help from Vickers. About half a dozen staff of the x-ray department went on a rota basis of six weeks each.

The accommodation was in Nissen huts and known as Boston Camp. I was housed in Block 2 Room 6, which was a mile away from the Dounreay site. The conditions would be considered unacceptable today but we were provided with all the basic necessities and there was a homely atmosphere. We had a canteen, a bar and a special room for watching a black-and-white television. I watched the first ever episode of *Steptoe and Son*, a drama series of a rag-and-bone man and his son there. The water in the taps was always brown, coming as it did from the surrounding peaty land.

The work involved 12-hour shifts seven days a week. This was well paid and allowed me to save quicker than normal.

This period of six weeks was the only time I grew a beard, and before I returned to England I had it shaved of by a barber in Thurso. My colleague, Arthur Burns, and I had been allowed to use the company Land Rover to go into Thurso. We had been on site for six weeks working our daily 12-hour shifts and we wanted to get one or two things for home. I decided to have a shave. I asked the barber, "Do you do shaves?" and he said yes. He started lathering me up using clean towels to wipe away the excess and then proceeded with his cut-throat razor. It seemed to take ages and a few men who were waiting for haircuts eventually left. I thought, this is going to cost a lot of money. I said "How much?" and he replied, "One and sixpence", and I repeated, in bewilderment at the low price, "One and sixpence [7.5p]?" and he said, "Yes, I had to heat the water, my friend." Arthur Burns who was waiting for me could not believe it. It was the best shave I have ever had.

Moving On

I returned to my farming activities at Urswick which involved carrying out routine duties including feeding the chickens and turkeys for Christmas. Brian with his marketing skills suggested to me that as I had my contacts at Vickers why didn't I take orders for his home-produced turkeys and chickens. I soon built up clients there and I delivered on the day before Christmas by taking a day of annual leave. Brian paid me one shilling in the pound (5 per cent) and I enjoyed the social activity of it, and even received small Christmas boxes from some of my customers.

Brian and I would talk about the issues of the day, including business and finance. One of the debates I recall was whether you should install central heating in your house. Brian came to the conclusion it would be cheaper to put a small electric radiator in each room but this overlooked the benefit of ease of use and the value added to your house.

My widowed auntie Edith (Shuttleworth) who lived behind us at Craglands was interested in moving to Ulverston and was going to sell her house. It was offered to me for £1,500 pounds. I gave it some thought and on reflection it would have been a good buy. However I was rather indecisive and let the opportunity go, always fearing of over committing myself. Plus I don't think Doreen was overly impressed with the idea of living in Urswick; she preferred an Ulverston location.

Doreen's two elder sisters Marjorie and Joyce were already married to farmers and Walter, her brother, was to be married to Eileen Edmundson in 1961. Eileen was an Ulverston girl who was in the same class as me at secondary school. By parental agreement Walter and his wife Eileen moved into the farm, at which point Doreen's mother and father bought a house called "Sunny Brow" in Spark Bridge for their retirement. Carole, Doreen's younger sister who was still at school, also moved with her parents to Spark Bridge.

A house came on the market in Ulverston. Number 14, Lightburn Avenue: a three-bedroom, terraced house with a small front garden and a 16ft x 8ft "Kencast" prefabricated garage situated a few yards outside the property in the back street. The rear of the house faced onto the park. It was to be sold by auction.

The house was in a handy location in the town and close to public transport and was situated about half way between Urswick and Colton, which is why I was interested in buying it.

This was to be my first experience of buying through auction and I was well aware that if the auctioneer's hammer went down on my bid it would be mine and all the financing had to be in place or found in a very short time.

It was on the evening of 8ᵗʰ May 1962 that I went along to the sale room of the auctioneers, F.J. Harrison and Son, in County Square, Ulverston, with Brian Wood as my mentor.

The bidding started slowly but was knocked down to my bid of £2,500. I thought it was about 5 per cent above the going rate. However, the house became mine through the help of Halifax Building Society. Through my prudence I had managed to save enough for a deposit of £1,000 which was quite an achievement – 40 per cent of cost, all earned and saved by myself – but there were also the legal fees and the contribution to any furnishings to consider.

Even with this amount of deposit the building society wanted more in the form of a guarantee because the valuers put a lower price on the property than what was paid. I think it was 85 per cent, so they wanted an extra insurance premium for the rest.

At the time some of Doreen's family friends were Mr and Mrs Lawrenson who visited the farm at Colton at holiday times and week-ends. He had his own accountancy practice in Barrow and said if I had any queries to go and see him. When the extra guarantee was required I discussed it with him and he approached the building society to say I was putting more down than he could and the building society duly decided to waiver the extra insurance premium.

After the house was bought and prior to moving in I had a further spell working away at Dounreay, and Doreen tells me she had everything in place including the decoration when I came back, and the only thing I did was paint the back door. This was a great underestimation of the duties I fulfilled.

Our marriage was arranged for 10th November 1962 at Colton Parish Church. The timing of the event had to fit in with the farming calendar cycle as the family were too busy in the spring and hay timing in summer so November was about the best option.

Planning for this event went well. The bridesmaids were my sister Enid and Joan Harris who was a friend of Doreen's family who used to stay with her parents in the area for holidays and came from Waterfoot, Rosssendale, in East Lancashire. At the time Joan was a buyer for a major merchandising company in London (Jax stores) and now has a real estate business in Johannesburg. Walter was my best man; Doreen's younger sister Carole and Jane Boyren and Marion Wood were flower girls and my cousin John Park and Doreen's cousin Myras Casson were groomsmen. The reception took place at the Sun Hotel in Coniston, a place we used to frequent. Connie Robinson, the proprietor, was well known to my wife's family because Doreen's grandparents and uncle farmed at Coniston Hall. The number of wedding lunches was 69 and the price per head was 12/6 pence. A bus was laid on for the guests who didn't have transport (see Appendix J).

The wedding service was arranged by the Rev. Thomas Stanton who was getting on in years and who lived in the large vicarage below the church. When I went to the vicarage to pay him the fee for the wedding he seemed a bit muddled and placed the bundle of pound notes I had given him behind an old vase on the mantlepiece, and I thought to myself he may misplace this. So in my scepticism I asked him for a receipt which I don't remember whether he gave to me or not because Doreen was pounding my ear that I shouldn't doubt a vicar's sincerity. I always felt that money control and traceability should be practised at whatever level. This can clarify any confusion or doubt that may arise later.

Following the wedding reception we travelled to Ulverston railway station to catch the mid-afternoon train to Euston for our week-long honeymoon in London. As we boarded the train we met another local couple who had just been married that day too. They were Ray Rushforth and Emily Hool and coincidentally Emily was a farmer's daughter and Ray a metallurgist at the steelworks. Ray became a work colleague of mine when he joined Vickers from the redundancy programme at Barrow steelworks. Ray and Emily still live locally and we sometime reminisce.

For our honeymoon we stayed in Room 3019 at The Royal Hotel, Woburn Place, Russell Square, for a charge of 52/- (£2.60) for two, and were situated a few hundred yards from Euston Station and well positioned for the sites and theatres of London.

We saw most of the sights of London, attended the Remembrance Service at the Cenotaph on a very cold and muggy day, and enjoyed some shows in the West End including Bruce Forsyth, Teddy Johnson and Pearl Car, Morecambe and Wise, and Eve Boswell, who were all performing.

We attended *West Side Story* and, at the Duchess Theatre, a play called *Good Night Mr Puffin*, and also enjoyed a farce with Brian Rix at the Whitehall Theatre. Later on in my life I had the pleasure of sitting opposite Brian on a train to London. He was then Lord Rix and was travelling for his duties in the House of Lords. He still had time to tell me prior to my taking my seat on the train that he had been travelling from Hull and how he had arranged for the train to stop at an earlier station to allow a man who was having some chest pains to get help. He contacted the stationmaster and had first-aid facilities made available. When Lord Rix got off at Euston he had his chauffeur pick him up while I had to wait in a long queue for a taxi.

Doreen and I returned from our honeymoon and began to build the foundations for our own family and my working life. I had steady, meaningful employment, a house, a loving and supportive wife; this was a good platform to build on.

I still had doubts on how things would work out but a structure which I considered manageable was in place.

1. *My parents' wedding, 1934, at Bank End*

2. *My mother with her parents at Bank End*

3. *My mother with my sister and me at Bank End*

4. *Top: My sister and me in our pram*
5. *Above: Me as a baby, in the garden,
with Tinker's Row behind*
6. *Right: Me aged about 8 years old*

7. *Above: Bank End, Great Urswick, taken by Leslie Sansom, 1940s*

8. *Below: 1 Bank End, Great Urswick, taken with a Box Brownie, c. 1958*

9. *1 Bank End Terrace, Great Urswick, 1960, taken with Rolliflex*

10. *40 Rusland Crescent, 2007 (one of my first digital photos)*

11. *Left to right: My sister, George Woodall, Tony the dog, Bill Woodall and myself*

12a and 12b. *Below, left and right: Me and my sister on Bardsea beach*

13. *Over the garden gate. Me, my father, my sister, my mother*

URSWICK GRAMMAR SCHOOL 1948

14. *Urswick Grammar School, 1948*
Back row: Brian Fisher, Geoff Robinson, Stan Fisher, Jimmy Steel
Next row: Joan Hinchy, Lesley Chapman, Kathleen Galbraith, Arthur Slater,
Brian Hurford, Miss Dobson
Next row: Yvonne Campbell, Audrey Goodall, Betty Postlethwaite, June
Lattimer, Barbara O'Connor, Dorothy Stables, Jean Hudson
Front row: June Stamford, me, Lily Postlethwaite, Arnold Slater, Mary
O'Connor, Brian Lambert and George Woods

15. *Me in soapbox,*
"Ossick Coot"

16. *Urswick Sea Scouts*
with "Ossick Coot"
soapbox at Salford Back:
Mr Grieve (Rev.),
Raymond Wilkinson,
Irving Gowling
Middle row: Lawrence
Robinson, Gavin Shields,
Jimmy Steel
Front row: Jimmy
Mossop, me, Maurice
Oldcorn (in car), Terry
Edmondson

17. *Part of the inter-school cross-country team. Left to right: me, Gordon Long, Alvin Hewitson, Gordon Lyle, Headley Potts*

18. *Urswick Sea Scouts on Urswick Tarn, late 1940s*

19. *Urswick Sea Scouts. Back, seated, l to r: Tom Neilson, Lawrence Robinson, James Jackson, Tom Jackson, Jimmy Steel, Michael Townson; front, standing: James Pattinson, Michael Jackson*

20. *Urswick Sea Scouts, manouvering a lock, canal camping week*

CHAPTER FOUR

1963–1979

Aged 23–40 Years

Marriage, Children, Supervisor

"My hair froze solid"

After our wedding we settled into our stone built, three-bedroom terraced house which was well situated for access to the bus station, the railway station and within walking distance of the town centre. Doreen continued to help her brother's wife Eileen at the farm in Colton three days a week, travelling from Ulverston to Greenodd by bus where she was picked up by Eileen for the 2-mile journey on to the farm.

I made the use of my NSU Quickly, a 50cc moped, to travel to work. This served me well but after our marriage I bought my first car, a 1,000 cc grey Morris, registration number 393 GTE, which I bought from Henry Miller in the Gill in Ulverston for £275.

The garage at the house was let out to an insurance man who lived round the corner in Conishead Road. Mrs Athersmith, the previous owner of the house, had let it to him and after the sale he asked me if he could carry on making use of it. I said yes under the condition that if and when I got a car I would want it back. He was quite happy with this arrangement and when the time came he would vacate the garage.

On vacating the garage he duly knocked on the door and said to my wife, "Tell your dad I have swept the garage out and thank him very much." The wife just laughed and said, "He is not my dad, he's my husband!"

When I bought the car I decided to go for a bank loan and approached the then District Bank, now the National Westminster, on the top of Queen Street overlooking the market square in Ulverston. I made an appointment and was shown into the manager's office which overlooked the market square. It was a large office and what was noticeable was that he was seated behind a large polished desk and the only piece of paper on show was the one that was applicable to me and my request. There were a few *Farmer and Stockbreeder* magazines with other publicity leaflets placed alongside in a rack at the side. Other than this it was a large open space.

This was to me an indication of the apparent efficiency in the way the bank worked. Besides all the important things and papers the manager had to deal with, the time he allocated for me was for me and me only; he was focussed on one task at a time. This impression has stayed with me, though I have never successfully emulated such efficiency.

The only question I remember him asking was "How are you going to service this loan?" At the time I didn't quite understand what he meant. As I was pondering he said, "Out of income?" and I said yes. This was my first introduction to my own banking arrangements and I have stayed with the bank to this day.

Life for the next few years was a case of Doreen and me settling down together and the next major event was the birth of our first child, a girl, Susan Carole, on 22nd February 1965. This event tended to make our lives more complete.

It was in 1966 that we decided to move house. The house we had in Lightburn Avenue was a good, substantial house, but it had its limitations and Doreen expressed an interest in a bungalow with some garden and access to schools. There was a company developing a new housing estate in the Croftlands area called GCT Construction, later known as Barnes, after the building contractor Derek Barnes who had his head office in Blackburn. Doreen approached the site agent but at the time the first section of build was oversubscribed but due to the building requirements of the local council they couldn't develop one corner of the site as intensively as they thought and subsequently they had to fit a smaller number of larger bungalows in an area in which they'd intended to build a larger number of smaller ones. This was being finalised as we made our approach. We looked at the plans and location: the lay out was a three-bedroom, semi-detached bungalow with an integral garage with garden to the front, rear and side. We decided we would buy. The plot was number 14, to become 40 Rusland Crescent. The price quoted was £3,395. Over time we've carried out a few modifications to the structure of the house: converting the garage into a bedroom and one of the bedrooms into a dining room, dropping the curb, building a garage at the rear and a conservatory. It has been our home ever since.

This meant we had to sell our existing house which we did through F.J. Harrison and Sons Auctioneers in Ulverston, the auctioneers we had originally bought it through. This was another experience for me having to watch your house being subject to a bidding process. The amount it sold for was £2,800, a £300 increase on the price I'd bought it for. Although acceptable, its value hadn't increased as much as other properties being sold. This then required an alteration to our mortgage which became £2,700 over 25 years at an interest rate of 7.26 per cent, total payment of £19-10-7, every calendar month.

We moved into the bungalow on the 10th December 1966. At the time Doreen was expecting our second baby, David Robert, who was born on the 3rd April 1967.

This was at a time when a number of young families were moving into the Crescent. It became a very pleasant locality with good friendships and atmosphere amongst the young families and children, though there were the odd elderly couple too, but it became a homogenous community of family life, with good access to Ulverston, to schools and to the local pub, The Lancastrian.

Some time later The Lancastrian became the meeting place of the Ulverston Organ Society of which I was a member. Representatives of Crane & Son Ltd (for everything musical) of Preston came each week to teach people how to play the organ. They brought with them a different model of organ each time. What emerged was the publicity and marketing technique that went along with what just seemed to be a genuine learning experience. It wasn't long before members got talking to each other and one or two had bought an organ from the company, and as time went on they traded for a higher specification model and theirs became available for somebody else. The only thing I bought a small, electric, portable model for £16 which can be used in confined areas having only a four-octave range with small keys. The volume control was operated by moving your knee sideways against a lever.

If this marketing exercise was being carried out on other nights of the week in other places then it was a very useful and practical marketing technique which lead to increased organ playing in the early 1970s.

In November 1967 I was called to do a longer spell – approximately nine months – at Dounreay and I thought I would try and take the family with me.

One of the Vickers staff at Dounreay was vacating a detached bungalow out at Dunnet Head and I managed to get the tenancy for the last seven months of the period I was there. Although I was working 12-hour days, this was a very exciting and adventurous period. Going home to the family each night was brilliant. Doreen didn't mind the loneliness and remoteness because she had the few villagers around her and the village post lady, Jenny.

The locals greeted us with open arms, especially with having two young children, and we were only a few hundred yards from a well-established pub and restaurant, the Northern Sands. The landlord's son was very into Scottish nationalism which meant rather delicate conversations, especially when England was playing Scotland at football. This was a location where I enjoyed a pint of Guinness.

Travelling up to Thurso with the family was quite dramatic and I retell the story from my notes I made at the time.

The bungalow was named "Dunedin". It was in an isolated position in the village of Dunnet, 20 miles east of Dounreay and 12 miles west of John-o-Groats and was fully furnished, including a telephone, telephone number Barrock 604. The property belonged to a widowed woman, Mrs Fergus, who lived at 6 Mary Street, Paisly, but any business was arranged and dealt with by her daughter, Mrs Cameron, who lived at 1 St. Peters Road, Thurso.

The rent for the bungalow was £10 per week, which at the time was rather expensive but with the scarcity of furnished accommodation available, combined with a large number of people after them, I would have had to pay just a little less for a far inferior property.

It was arranged for the whole family, which consisted of myself, Doreen, our daughter Susan, who was nearly three, and our 9-month-old son, David, to travel by car on 2nd January 1968. My car at the time was a Austin 1300, registration number EEO 133 E (May 1967). The journey was arranged to take two full days, covering approximately 250 miles each day. On the morning of the 2nd a light snow had fallen, not enough to make the ground white but I contacted the Automobile Association (AA) to enquire about the road conditions further north. They reported that snow had fallen over northern England and south west Scotland but the roads were clear to traffic.

The car was heavily laden. The contents consisting of a television set in the alcove behind the driver's seat. The rear seat was piled high with blankets and David's carry-cot secured on top of the blankets and television. The carry-cot was positioned forward to aft and David actually travelled in the carry-cot in this position sleeping most of the time. Susan had the remainder of the rear seat to sleep and play. The rear window ledge was overflowing with equipment. The boot of the car contained numerous large polythene bags of children's clothes and nappies. Fortunately the baby trolley had been taken by Peter Turnbull (from The Gill, Ulverston) in his Ford Anglia estate car, and a large trunk containing bedding and winter overcoats had been collected prior to Christmas by a Vickers lorry and delivered to the Dounreay site for collection later. The roof rack on my car carried two large suitcases and Susan's toy pram. Combined with all this was the weight of the four passengers, so the car was heavily laden. This had its advantages later on the journey!

We commenced our journey from Ulverston at approximately 9.15 am, leaving Mrs Phillipson (Doreen's mother) to clear up behind us.

The journey was uneventful for the first hour. Susan kept asking, "Are we here now?" She was sick just south of Carlisle, so we had to remove her anorak and trousers, and she continued the journey with a blanket wrapped around her. The sick-covered clothing was placed in the boot of the car.

On the journey through the English lakes the hills were all covered with snow but by lunch time it had started to rain. Once over the border into Scotland the weather improved, with intermittent outbreaks of sunshine, but the A74 road was quite slushy, giving the impression that rather more snow had fallen than in England.

We stopped for a midday meal at the Beatock House Hotel at Beatock, turning left off the A74. I also obtained some petrol which was rather difficult because it being New Year's day, Scotland was still in the throes of feasting and merriment. Anyway I persuaded the garage proprietor to open up the pump and fill my tank. He mentioned that he had had difficulty in travelling home in his car during the night owing to the bad snow storms.

My intention for the day's journey was to arrive at Perth before dark and settle into a hotel. Perth was approximately halfway between Ulverston and Thurso. It was just 4.30 pm when we arrived in Perth and we booked into the Royal George Hotel, Tay Street. A double room with a double bed and one single bed was allocated, with David sleeping in his carry-cot. The night was fairly peaceful, David awaking at midnight, but a drink of boiled water relieved him of the wind that was troubling him and everything was well until the morning.

On rising out of bed and looking out of the hotel bedroom window, which faced the river Tay, I got a sudden shock, for there outside was a blanket of snow about three inches deep. I thought, just my luck travelling through the Grampian Mountains today.

We made our way out of Perth at approximately 9.30 am and onto the A9 going north. On the outskirts of the town there was a large police notice saying "Road Blocked Blair Atholl for 11 Miles". Parked by the notice was a police car. I stopped and asked the police officer in the car what the situation was. While asking him a message came over his radio saying the A9 was now open and the traffic was moving, but very slowly. With Blair Atholl being some 30 miles further north I decided to carry on the journey, hoping the road situation would ease as the day went on.

We progressed very slowly, mainly in third gear, although no further snow had fallen whilst we were travelling. As we approached Blair Atholl large drifts on either side of the road indicated the snow plough had worked to clear the road. The drifts were with us for 15 miles.

Going through Dalwhinie, where I expected trouble, the roads were clear. The council had salted them and there was no indication of snow on the road. Around 11.45 am we were passing Aviemore. David's feed was due at about 12.30 pm and with Inverness being only some 30 miles further north we decided to press on and have lunch there.

On passing through Carbridge we overtook a large furniture removal van when all of a sudden the wind got up. The wind was at least gale force hitting us broadside from the passenger side. The snow was being blown across the road and a blizzard started. I battled on until the visibility was nil and as a last resort I tried driving with my head out of the hand-held open door. The snow rushed in, wetting the pile of blankets and the car interior. It came to the point we could travel no further and with the car being wet inside now it was going to be very uncomfortable to stay in it. By this time the furniture van we'd overtaken at Carbridge was directly behind us. So I asked the driver if we could get in his cab. He agreed. By now the snow was coming horizontally with no visibility.

The driver of the van was taking furniture just north of Inverness for a doctor from the south of England. The blizzard never let up for two hours and by then my car was completely covered in snow and the south bound traffic had been trapped some 50 yards further ahead.

On the occasional visit I made to my car in the early stages of the blizzard to collect coffee and biscuits my hair froze solid and my overcoat froze on me and my hands went numb. When Susan saw me she began crying with fright and David cried too because it was well past his feed time. The driver of the furniture van had enough fuel to keep the engine running and to provide heat for twenty-four hours. Nevertheless the van cab windows remained frozen inside and out. My coat and hair began to thaw making it very uncomfortable for me.

It was over two and half hours after stopping and still snowing when a knock came on the side of the van driver's door. A man asked if the car in front, which was mine, could be moved so they could get the snowplough through. I went to the car and managed to get the driver's door open but inside there were icicles hanging from the steering wheel. I thought, this will never start and if it did I would never get it out of the deep snow piled up around the car.

I pulled the choke cable full out and then turned the starter motor and it started first time. I managed to square the car to allow the passage of the plough. Once the plough went by I followed it directly hoping the furniture van with my family would be able to follow. Once I was moving I didn't want to stop. Looking in my mirror I saw the van following. What a relief.

Of the traffic coming south the third vehicle was a police car. They had probably been responsible for calling for the plough to come to our assistance.

I followed the plough until it turned off about 15 miles south of Inverness. I carried on as the trail leader of a convoy of vehicles for another two miles, until I approached a bend where several cars had been left stranded and one was just being abandoned. There was just enough room for a single vehicle to pass through, with drifts of snow and cars on either side. I knew I could get through but was unsure about the furniture van with my wife and family on board because of its length.

I waited until the furniture van caught up and I then asked the driver if he could get through the gap. Whilst talking, my wife drew my attention and gave the impression she wanted to get out. The driver said he would be able to get through the gap and I said I would relieve him of my family and thanked him for the help and for providing shelter for us.

My wife mentioned she had been extremely worried whilst in the cab. When she offered to wipe his windows with a rag from the back of her seat a gun dropped out of the rag. Also the driver appeared semi-literate; he couldn't understand the map he was looking at and he had no idea were he was.

On passing through the gap between the abandoned cars and the drifts a large lorry travelling south was coming head-on to us. I had to turn sharp left into a colossal snow drift to avoid the lorry. This completely encased the bonnet of the car in the snow. Not only were we stuck but the furniture van's rear wheels were spinning to try and get traction with no avail. Fortunately, some workmen from the adjacent railway line, who were clearing the line of snow, dug us out and enabled us to carry on with our journey to Inverness. The last three-and-a-half hours were the most frightening of my life. We arrived in Inverness at 4.30 pm, having taken seven hours to cover 113 miles.

We booked into the Cummings Hotel and were treated very well because of our ordeal and especially with a young family. First thing to be done was to get changed into something dry, and then have something to eat. While sitting in the lounge after all getting changed Susan accidentally knocked my pint of beer onto my trousers, so I had to get changed again.

Susan and I had our meal in the restaurant but my wife didn't feel up to it because of the traumatic journey. Nevertheless the hotel management insisted on taking something to her room. We went to bed early but nobody had any sleep. David cried all night and Susan did her best to sleep through it.

The following morning no more snow had fallen but it had frozen very hard. The radio weather report indicated that the roads in Caithness were chaotic. So I telephoned the AA and they said there was hard-packed snow all the way from Inverness to Thurso, but if we took care, especially on corners, we should be ok.

I telephoned my site manager (Peter Lister) who was already at Thurso to say that I had been delayed because of snow and depending on the road conditions I would try and make it to Thurso that day. He told me not to worry; apparently I wasn't the only one who hadn't made it. They themselves had been caught in a blizzard further north at Helmsdale and had to abandon their car and carry out the remainder of their journey by train, collecting their car the following weekend.

On leaving the hotel I opened the bonnet of the car to check the oil level and the entire engine compartment was completely covered in frozen snow except for the area around the spark plug leads where the leads join the plugs. The snow, plenty of which had come through the radiator grill during the blizzard, had formed a complete mould of the engine

We set off for Thurso, travelling along the coastal route via Tain and Wick to avoid the more direct but hilly route over the Struie Pass. Just before lunch time snow started to fall again, no blizzard, just a steady fall of large flakes. We travelled on until we arrived at Bonar Bridge. We stopped at a hotel for lunch where the proprietor made us a special meal but with the worry of more snow and associated problems we didn't eat much, only the soup. The proprietor advised us to travel to Helmsdale, which was some miles away, and stay the night at the Bridge Inn. She knew the owner well and would telephone ahead and book us in. Apparently the previous night they had had people sleeping in the corridor in the hotel. I thanked her kindly and said we would progress as far as we could for we might not even reach Helmsdale. Around 2.30 pm we arrived in Helmsdale and enquired at the Bridge Inn if the road over the Ord to Caithness was passable. He told me traffic had been coming through and that is all he could say. I decided to chance it. The snow over the Ord was several inches thick but with the extra weight of the car we managed to get over, occasionally spinning on the tight bends and inclines.

The journey to Wick was very treacherous and we arrived there at 4.30 pm. By then it was getting dusk and even though we had got to Wick there was still a further 30 miles west to Thurso. We arrived at Thurso at about 5.15 pm and called on Mrs Cameron to collect the key. She had prepared our bungalow at Dunnet. She and her family welcomed us and provided us with an excellent meal; they had worried about us on our journey. After the meal we left for Dunnet which was eight miles east of Thurso and arrived at the bungalow at 6.30 pm. Mrs Cameron had left an electric fire on for us.

The car was unloaded and I fixed the television, which we had brought along, into position but when I switched it on there was a hissing and sizzling noise, so I switched it off and let it dry out overnight. We all retired to bed to begin our seven months' stay in the north of Scotland.

Prior to this journey north I had had an experience coming home from Thurso to Ulverston in the week before Christmas while travelling with my colleague, Joe Knight.

Joe and I had been doing work at Dounreay and we had intended to travel home the following day. After finishing our shift we got back to the hotel at about 8.00 pm and decided we would travel down that evening and through the night instead of waiting until morning. Grabbing a quick snack at the hotel and picking up our belongings we set off south more or less as we were and unshaven.

Although the temperature was near freezing the journey was fine until we met the junction of the A836 with the Struie' pass, the B9176 that goes over the higher ground and the longer journey around the coast via Tain. I asked Joe whether we should chance going over the Struie and in the hesitation I touched my brakes and the car slid on black ice into the rough triangular section at the junction. There was quite a noticeable collision. I then reversed slowly and slid into the banking on the side of the road. Joe had a toy piano on the back parcel shelf of the car which was for his daughter as a Xmas present, this came tumbling and tingling down onto the rear seat and floor. I said, that's the front end bashed in and also the back end. We didn't get out to inspect the damage because it was too dark. However we decided to go along the coast road which was still slippery. We met a car coming head-on to us at a bridge which was only wide enough for a single vehicle at a time. Somehow we managed to keep the two cars apart and Joe said, how did I do that and I said I don't know but I'm going no further tonight. There in the distance were some lights of a cottage or farm house and I said let's try there.

As we went along the road conditions eased and softened so we decided to travel very slowly to Inverness and try and get accommodation, which may not have been easy at that time of night.

We pulled into the street parking opposite the Cummings Hotel in Inverness at about 10.00 pm and managed to get two rooms. We decided to have a quick drink at the bar and then retire. Whilst at the bar I mentioned to Joe that I had better straighten up or move the car because I had parked rather hastily and it was sticking out beyond the white lines. I made it safe and then retired.

We had arranged for an early breakfast which the hotel provided and we were on the move at about 6.15 am. When leaving the hotel rooms a cleaner happened to say, "You lads are early this morning!"

and Joe said, "Yes you have to be on our job."

As we came out of the hotel towards our car I noticed the hotel manager was following behind and I thought he was an early riser too. He pretended to get into the car behind ours.

We duly travelled home without any further incident, arriving home in the late afternoon.

The man who lived across the road from me, Trevor Wolfenden, came over to me and said he had had a visit from the police the previous night enquiring whether I had some dogs for training. I thought no more about it until later that evening when Joe rang me and said, "Did your wife have a visit from the police last night?" and I said, "No," and he said his wife was knocked up and asked whether she knew where her husband was and what he was doing. She said he was working away for Vickers and was due home any time soon. The police would tell her no more and left her upset. I said my wife wasn't knocked up, but the police had enquired across the road if I had some dogs to train.

I said I was not happy with this and would go down to the police station in Ulverston to see what was happening.

I went into the police station and asked at the desk whether they wanted some dogs for training. The constable said, "I don't know. I will get you the dog handler." I asked the dog handler whether he was looking for some dogs to train and he replied, "Why? Have you got some?" I said, "No, I've never had a dog in my life. Who told you I had some?" He replied, "A pal of yours." I asked for the name of this pal but he refused to give this information. I said, "I want to see the superintendent," and he replied, "You can't because he's at a function at the Old Mill at Bardsea." "Well in that case," I said, "I will be in to see him in the morning."

In the morning I explained to the superintendent what had gone on. He explained that they had received a report from Inverness police about two "suspect characters" in the Cummings Hotel. They were asked to confirm that I lived at the address I had provided the hotel. The superintendent said that where I lived was a relatively newly built estate and we were not yet on the electoral role, so he had to find out if I lived at 40 Rusland Crescent, which he did as unobtrusively as possible by enquiring across the road.

I said, "That's fine; my wife wasn't disturbed and you probably got the information you required. However, the wife of my colleague at Barrow was knocked up with no explanation." He said that was just bad "bobby-ing" and it shouldn't have happened. He said there would be an apology coming from Inverness police, which was never forthcoming.

Apparently the barman at the hotel had overheard our conversation about moving the car and the fact that both Joe and I are very dark and we may have had a bit of stubble made him suspicious and he had put the wheels in motion.

On my return journey with the family in the New Year and having to stay there because of the snow, I asked the barman if he remembered me. He just blushed and looked guilty. No doubt this may have been one of the reasons my family and I received exceptional treatment and comfort in our overnight stay.

Returning to my work in Barrow I continued to be an active member of a busy and progressive department. What I liked about the work was the involvement with most of the products the company produced, especially on the manufacturing and engineering side, and that it covered aspects of design, prototypes, and manufacturing and in service inspection commitments. It gave me a great sense of involvement, which perhaps in an office or more sedentary job where the work was more limited and ring-fenced, you wouldn't have. I came into contact with personnel from other departments, including labourers, tradesmen, managers and directors. This provided me with the chance to increase my social skills of understanding and working with people.

The department was expanding both in facilities and personnel, and being a relatively new inspection process there were not many readily trained personnel available so the department had to recruit both internally and externally to be trained in Non-Destructive Testing methods. Many of these recruits were tradesmen from within the company including joiners, plumbers, builders, electricians as well as white-collar staff, but some were being made redundant from other local industries including the ironworks, the railways and British Cellophane. All interviewees had to have the ability to be trained and also bring along their inherent skills and experiences from their previous jobs. They were of all ages and offered many skills though not directly related to NDT. This brought together different types of thinking and application, producing a synergy that drove the department. It was a male-dominated industry and the few women recruited had clerical and cleaning duties.

Training happened on the job, covering the specific disciplines of Radiography, Ultrasonic and Surface-Flaw Detection. The training provided was supplemented with externally approved courses and the operators were assessed in a similar way to the NVQ standards of today. National standards of competency in specific tasks were later introduced and operators were graded 1, 2 or 3, Grade 3 being the basic and starting grade that all trainees had to begin at if they had not the necessary skills. Other experienced people were brought in at the higher grades but this was limited to vacancies arising in those grades.

One of the trainees who was taken on as an assistant was Peter Brady. Peter was a plumber with Barrow Borough Corporation and was in his early twenties. He had got word on the grapevine that Vickers were recruiting in the "x-ray department" and Peter saw and took the opportunity by leaving the Corporation to join our department.

Peter was a likeable person full of humour, a prankster with built-in discipline from doing national service. In the few years he was with us he was trained in industrial radiography. It was at the time when people were emigrating to Canada and Australia, especially the young ones looking for other opportunities and a better life. Peter emigrated from England to Canada with his wife and built on his industrial radiography training. After a few years working in Canada with various companies he bought into an NDT company, ATLAS Inspection, and eventually became president of the Canadian Non-Destructive Society. His affable personality must have helped his progress. He was a good example of a person who changed direction and capitalised on it, and he said that once when standing in front of 2,000 delegates at a world conference he thought to himself what would "Lile Blackie" and Brian Lennon think of him now, delivering a speech in such a setting.

It was my good fortune to meet up with Peter whilst I was on holiday in Canada (in May 1996). Peter picked us up from the Bond Palace Hotel, Dundas Street, Toronto, where my wife and I were staying for two nights. This arrangement was made by letter three months earlier and without any further contact in walked Peter to collect us. Dressed in a shell suit he was still totally recognisable despite the 30 years since I had last seen him. His mannerisms and approach were exactly as I had known him. Peter took us to his house in Burlington where we met up with his wife, Ruth. Another Barrowvian, Brian Smith, and his wife, were also there. Peter and his wife Ruth served us an excellent barbeque and Peter also took us to visit his NDT company premises at 389 Davis Road, Oakville, Ontario. He duly returned us to the hotel that evening.

During our visit he recollected the time when he got the job with Vickers and when he applied he was told the position had been filled, but Peter would not take no for an answer and persuaded Mr Oldham, the Chief Chemist and Metallurgist, that he was the man for the job and somebody who had been previously interviewed and selected was substituted by Peter. This approach went with him through his life and he has got to be admired for demonstrating how a positive approach and personality can take you a long way. Other Barrowvians emigrated to Canada at the same time, and over the years were involved in a Barrow convention each year in Canada. Some of the others included Stan Slater, Brian Ward, Brian Smith, Mervyn Brown, David Anderson known as "Angus", and Mike Pates.

Of the older people who were taken on as assistants in our department, one person who stood out for me was Harry Rea. Harry was twenty years older than me and had come from a senior NDT and welding inspection supervisory role with Whesso Ltd, a large engineering and fabrication company based in Darlington.

Harry was a Barrowvian and wanted to return to Barrow. He was prepared to take a lower position to that he had been used to. He was employed as a radiographer. He already had two brothers working in Vickers, Hughie, an electrical manager, and Bill, a manager in personnel or the "labour department" as it was then known.

Harry fitted in well as part of my team which was responsible for radiography on welds of welded pipe sub assemblies in the temporary facilities known as the "Brick Shed". The shed contained sand bags and bricks which we made use of as a radiation shield to convert into radiographic compound for x-raying welds. We also made use of lead covered wooden screens to make doorways. This type of work was also carried out in the Old Billet Shed, as it was called, because it was a large building where steel billets used to be stored. By making use of concrete blast walls, this was a temporary radiographic facility with three x-ray compounds. This was prior to the Billet shed being turned into one of the largest x-ray and NDT facilities in the country. This facility was approximately 70 yards long and 40 yards wide and was designed out of a budget for the Polaris Nuclear submarine programme. Wilf Cotton made such a good job of the design and radiation calculations that the Factory Inspector who came to assess the work couldn't believe how much protection was built in. The Factory Inspector offered Wilf a position within the inspectorate but Wilf, being the modest man he was, declined. The area where the x-ray department stood in the North West Yard is now a borough park area along the channel side north of Walney Bridge.

Our small team consisted of me as a working supervisor, Harry, and three bright, young boys, Stuart Collins, Maurice Holliday and Fred Baker along with Ken Harper and Ted Callaghan. With these young spirited lads and Harry the more senior, mature person, the team worked well.

Harry became a big inspiration for me in how a supervisor should operate, bringing his experience of handling working situations on site and especially in personnel management. His communicating skills were second to none, both in written and verbal form. Harry always had an eye on improving his position in the company and it wasn't long before a position became available within the department.

The workload was increasing so much that the small team of

operators on night-shift had to expand and a night-shift supervisor had to be appointed. Harry was appointed to this position and carried it out very professionally.

It was normal for a detailed, written instruction to be left by the day-shift supervisor for the work that had to be carried out on the night-shift. Harry wouldn't accept this and said his position wasn't a sinecure and that the work should just be left to be done and he would allocate the men and resources accordingly. Quite right too; word was left for work to be done and within the limits of practicality Harry got it done, no matter who he stood on or upset in order to get the job done. Conversely if any of his night-shift operators were in trouble he would stand by them and put their case to management. He would sometimes refer to people as not having the sense to come in out of the rain. He always made sure his instructions back to the dayshift were duplicated for his own records and which he would frequently refer back to cover his own skin.

Because of its commitment to excellence the company was committed to training and development. It had its own training schools and encouraged employees to go on training courses, especially the apprentices who they had a vested interest in, but more senior people with an ambition for advancement were also encouraged but mainly in their own time in the evenings with an occasional half-day release.

In the early days most of the trade, technical and supervisory courses were run at the local technical college in Abbey Road and later at the College for Further Education in Howard Street.

One of these courses was the National Examination of Supervisory Studies (NEBSS) and was intended for potential and new supervisors and foremen. My colleague, Brian Lennon, was one of the first to enrol and it was due to his enthusiasm and encouragement that I enrolled the following academic year. I will always be grateful to Brian for having the foresight and for giving the lead that I perhaps might not have taken.

The course consisted of one half-day release (1.30 pm–4.30 pm) and an evening class (6 pm–9 pm) once a week. I began the course in September 1970. The syllabus covered Production Planning and Control, Finance and Accounts, Economics, Communication, Law and Industrial Relations. We also had project work which involved individual and group assignments and a written examination which was set and marked nationally.

The course tutor and senior lecturer was Ron Slater and other lecturers were from local industry, solicitors and accountants. Ron was very reserved and an academic. His lecturing skills were exemplary and his approach to delivering economic theory was a joy to experience. He certainly impressed me and gave me the understanding of business and industrial finance and this went for all the students on all his industrial management courses. After assessing one of my written assignments on personnel he wrote on the bottom of the page, "Thorough preparation and excellent writing. You are in the wrong job." This was an affirmation of my capabilities and I still periodically muse on it.

The NEBSS course was the catalyst for further management training, providing qualification for the Certificate in Industrial Management in the academic years 1971/72 and 1973/74 and the Diploma in Industrial Management in 1974/75. This was organised through the college and the Institute of Works Managers, now the Chartered Management Institute.

Ron was an iconic figure on all these courses and never got the full recognition he deserved.

The two year, part-time industrial management certificate course was an element of the Institute of Works Managers, now known as the Chartered Management Institute education programme, run through the accredited Barrow College of Further Education. It covered eight subjects: Works Management Theory and Practice, Economics of Industry, Psychology and Sociology, Statistics, Industrial Accounting, Industrial Law, Management Techniques, Works Manager and Personnel.

Success on this course gave you the right to apply for but not a guarantee of acceptance on the diploma course, with selection by interview. It was not just an extension of the certificate course but was an advanced course recognised as such by the Ministry of Education. The seven sections of the framework were: Investigating and Forecasting, Planning, Organising, Directing, Co-ordinating, Controlling and Communicating. These seven sections combined under one subject "Good Management".

Those who gained the diploma would be recognised, not only academically but in practice, and would also be able to fill a "fairly senior post in production management" (as my course notes indicate). This involved project work and the completion of a log book. You were finally interviewed by a panel for recommendation of a pass or a fail.

Following my success with the diploma and my acceptance as a corporate member of the Institute of Works Managers, I took up various committee roles in the Cumbrian branch of the Institute and finally became deputy chairman but chickened out when it came to the chairmanship because of other commitments. This was another example of my not wanting to be top dog, although other than this, I had all the qualities required. The expression comes to mind: "The higher up the tree the monkey goes the more it bares its arse", and I fell back to work around my natural frequencies or comfort zone.

As part of the Barrow Cumbria branch of the Institute of Works Managers we tried to get Ron recognised with membership but he was always turned down due to his lack of industrial experience. He was the man who helped most of the students to be recognised and gain a membership of the professional institution. I will always be grateful for what the College of Further Education provided, especially the business studies side. The head of the department at the time was David Kaine whom at the time I knew by name only, and from the odd appearance in class on one of his flying visits. It was only after leaving Vickers in 1994 that I met up with David and he became a mentor, confidant and sounding board for me in my involvement with the Prince's Trust, a charity that helps disadvantaged young people to start up in self-employment or business.

With the expanding NDT department it became a haven for students in their summer vacations to help with duties in the areas which were developing backlogs and delays. This was also an interesting and educative experience for graduate engineers, designers and naval architects to pass through as part of development for their future roles. I always advised the operators or technicians to make the trainees welcome and co-operate with their development. Many resented this saying it wasn't my job to teach these people. This negative approach was not encouraged. Training or showing people what you do is in everybody's interest and one day they may end up being your manager which on occasions did happen. The impression created would reflect on the department. It was this good relationship with these graduates and students that enhanced the department within the company, and also contributed in the areas of work the graduates were moving on to.

One of these graduates came from Australia and he was touring industries in the UK on a few months' programme. His surname was Keynes and he spent a few days in our North West shop facility where we radiographed welds on nuclear reactor components. I asked casually if he was related to Lord John Maynard Keynes, one of the most the brilliant economists of the twentieth century.

He replied, "Elleray, go to the top of the class. I have been in this country for several months and you are the first one to mention it. Yes I am a distant relation of John Maynard Keynes." (John Maynard Keynes was the noted English economist who believed that "government spending on public works is necessary to stimulate the economy" (*English Oxford Dictionary*). It was while studying economics that I was introduced to his theories.)

Another example of the company's encouragement of training was when we were working on part of a joint lightweight land gun contract with the Germans. We were encouraged to take German lessons to improve our working knowledge of the language. I think the specific intention was for us to gain some understanding of the technical German on drawings and specification documents, but the course was more like a general school course on the German language and we learnt nouns, verbs, adjectives, etc. and common phrases and how to make ourselves generally understood.

This was a one-year course of one evening per week at the College of Further Education. The teacher, Frau Sadler, delivered the course with feeling and empathy. As part of the course we had the opportunity to attend a two-week residential course at a school in Germany. One of the conditions was you took one week of your annual leave and the company would pay for the other. You were also allowed to take your wife.

The residential course took place from the 26th September to the 10th October 1970. The school was in the small village of Wiel der Stadt, a few miles southwest of Stuttgart in the Black Forest region.

My mother-in-law (Doreen's mother) agreed to look after our two small children, both still below school age, for this two-week period. Looking back, this was quite a commitment.

While at work Johnnie Bowyer rang me and said, "I believe you are going to Wiel der Stadt," and he asked me if he and his wife could get a lift with us. I said it would probably be ok but that I would discuss it with my wife. We agreed to take them, but he then asked whether we would be going the Hull–Rotterdam route and I said no we would be following the Dover–Ostend route. He argued that Hull–Rotterdam was the better way because he had been previously. I knew my wife would not be comfortable on the ferry across the North Sea and I said, "if you want to come with us we will be travelling via Dover." He duly agreed to this arrangement. But the journey was not without incident.

We travelled in my Austin 1300 green saloon car, my wife and I in the front and Mr and Mrs Bowyer in the back. We journeyed south to catch the ferry at Dover. Our first major stop was at a motorway service station on the M2 in Kent. Johnnie left his glasses behind there, but he said it was ok because he had another pair. This was to be a major factor in what was to come.

We boarded the ferry at Dover. Doreen and I had arranged for beds to sleep on the crossing; Johnnie and his wife, who were considerably older than us, had arranged for bucket-type chairs for resting. Before settling down for the night Johnnie said he would get a bottle of whiskey and I casually remarked, why a bottle of whiskey? He said just in case any body is ill on the course.

On arriving at Ostend we disembarked and made our way along the E2 towards Achan, stopping for a small breakfast by the roadside where Johnnie used his small primus stove to prepare a fry-up. We then approached the Belgium/German border point at Achaan where we had to hand over our passport for inspection. I handed both my wife's and mine over and then Johnnie passed theirs over but there was only one passport. Both were covered by the same one. We casually asked whether this was not a bit of a false economy and Mrs Bowyer said, "No anywhere Johnnie goes, I go with him."

We continued south, Johnnie directing me on the correct route because he had been before. When we came to a point on the German Autobahn where the road splits but with both routes heading south I asked Johnnie which one should I take. He hummed and hawed, and by the time he spoke I had already made the decision, but further on I thought I had better check and pulled into a service station to ask for guidance. Before I had managed to undo my seat belt Johnnie had rushed out to get guidance. Yes, we were on the correct road.

When we drove off Johnnie realised that when he rushed out of the car he had dropped his second pair of glasses. I said, "Ok Johnnie, I will pull over", and he got out and walked back. But the distance was deceptive we were on an arc moving away and above the petrol station. We could see where he had to go but it was further than he thought and he never made it to the station. He arrived back out of breath and his wife said this will not have done him any good. We moved off and it was only a few minutes later, when Doreen heard a gurgling noise as if Johnnie was sucking his pipe which he often used to do, that she realised there was something wrong, and she said, "Open his collar", but his wife remarked, "Ooh let him die in peace." On realising the seriousness of the situation we pulled off from the five-lane autobahn north of Kalsrue into a large shopping precinct. I parked the car and went for help. My wife was not able to speak German and gesticulated to some people by tapping her chest and saying "heart attack". They replied "fünf minuten!" and within five minutes there was an ambulance alongside the car. The ambulance men threw open the car door and felt Johnnie's pulse and they just shook their heads. They loaded him into the ambulance and as the ambulance was getting ready to move off Mrs Bowyer asked if I would go along in the ambulance with them and I said yes, but just let me shut and secure my car doors. In this short time the ambulance drew off without me. I asked the local police officers in attendance the direction to the hospital but it was too complicated and I could do no more.

My wife and I were rather stunned by the incident but said we would have to continue to Weil-der-Stadt which involved leaving the motorway and finding the small village 30 miles away down much narrower roads. I had been relying on Johnnie to provide the finer details of this journey because he had been before. Nevertheless we made it to the school and all the intake of the course were there to greet us, asking the obvious question: where's Johnnie and his wife? We had to announce the bad news and Herr Brennar, the head of the school, who was also high up in German politics, took over from us. He soon established Johnnie had been dead on arrival at the hospital. We stayed at the school for two weeks and thanks to Herr Brennar we were not approached about the incident. Through his diplomatic contacts he arranged to fly Mrs Bowyer home from Frankfurt airport and Johnnie's body returned on another flight. The fact they were both on the same passport caused great difficulties. If the body was to be flown back Mrs Bowyer would not be able to, and vice versa. It must have been resolved by Herr Brennar. Both Mrs Bowyer and the coffin eventually arrived home.

Whilst on the course I put the incident to the back of my mind but Doreen was fretful and upset about it.

We were later to establish that the reason Johnnie had asked to travel with us was because his previous colleagues wouldn't take him because of medical problems. Apparently he had already suffered two heart attacks and I thought it was a bit deceitful not to tell us the true situation. When filling the AA five-star insurance form I had put Johnnie down as having good health.

On returning to work I had to report on the event to the manager of Personnel, Fred Mather, and his secretary, Edith Hill. I had to explain what had happened, and the subject of insurance cover invariably came up. Before leaving for Germany I had arranged insurance through the AA's 5-star cover and had listed the passengers as my wife and Mr and Mrs Bowyer. I listed them as having no serious medical conditions, but on subsequent reflection on Johnnie's heart problem I worried that the insurance may have been null and void. However the procedure was that the costs associated with the death were invoiced to Vickers and I had to claim in the first instance all the other costs through my own insurance. The AA insurers were in the same group of insurers that covered all Vickers' insurance so there was a mutual benefit of working together.

All the monies came through me and I forwarded them to Vickers, items which included the airfares, the cost of a lead-lined coffin and embalming fees. Fred Mather said that I would be responsible for some costs. I said, not really, the only cost I was involved with was the cost of a telephone call home from Germany to tell our families there had been no accident and Johnnie had died through natural causes. But I then mentioned that Johnnie had agreed to pay half the petrol. I entered the 850-mile round trip on the claim form at the appropriate mileage and claimed the 50 per cent Johnnie had agreed to pay, and the claim was duly accepted.

This was a very sad event and gave me and my wife an experience that has stayed with us.

With the retirement in 1972 of Wilf Cotton, the manager of the Non-Destructive Testing department, there was a reorganisation of the department and I was appointed Senior Radiographer on the 1st March 1972, and Ken Norman was the new head of department, which had been incorporated into the Quality Control Department in 1965 instead of being part of the laboratory. This was because NDT was now considered part of inspection, quality control and assurance rather than the more applied aspects of testing within the laboratory. The overall manager was Noel Davies who was not long out of university and was being groomed for higher things in the naval nuclear reactor build programme. He eventual rose to be a director of Vickers Plc and was later knighted. He was a very approachable gentleman. This change meant a broadening of quality assurance and testing and we grew into a very big department employing around 300 personnel. My responsibilities covered all aspects of the radiography requirements of the engineering works alongside my colleagues Tony Slone who covered Ultrasonics, and Bill Postlethwaite who was in charge of Surface Flaw inspection.

There are times when you are in situations that you are not directly involved with but because of an association you are asked to act. This happened once when I was sent once again for a few days' spell to Dounreay and I had travelled up as an individual to carry out some radiographic inspection. I arrived at the Pentland Hotel in Thurso on a Friday morning after staying in Inverness overnight and aimed to travel out to site after lunch. In the hotel bar at the time were a couple of coppersmiths and one welder who had travelled up from Barrow on the sleeper train. They were Vickers' men but were to carry out their own work independently of me. They'd had a few drinks on the train journey and were in a happy disposition. They asked me if I was going to site and I said yes. They said, would you mind giving us a lift. I responded, yes, I would, but they had to behave themselves and reduce their jocularity. Oh yes, Geoff, we will not let you down, they replied. The main reason they had to travel to site was to formally report in and go through an induction process with the administration department which every visitor to site had to do. Your medical and radiation records were checked. Theses routine checks had to be in place for them to be able to work the weekend as pre-arranged from Barrow.

I drove them to site and they were reasonably behaved. We then went our different ways but we met up in the medical room where a nurse checked our personal details. We were in an orderly queue and one of the coppersmiths went to lean against what he thought was a hardboard petition divider in the clinic but it was a portable canvass screen which he then stumbled against and fell over. This caused a bit of a scene and the nurse went out to see the works medical officer, came back and beckoned to the coppersmith to come over and she took him to the medical officer. I returned to my office to prepare for the work I was to carry out.

Later I received a telephone call from the site Safety Officer demanding that I get this man off site. I argued that he had nothing to do with me, to which he replied, "You are the senior Vickers mans on site, get him off."

This was a bit embarrassing but, as he put it, I had this duty to perform. Not only was he asked to go but the other two were as well.

The site discipline imposed on them required that they stopped working on the Saturday and were only allowed to work on the Sunday. The disciplinary constraint could have been more dire; they could have been asked to return to Barrow. They argued all the way back to the hotel in the car that they were told they would be working *seven* days a week and they were going to get in touch with their boss at Barrow. I said, look you have got off lightly and just accept you have lost a few hours.

That Sunday evening in the hotel, following some time to reflect, they thanked me for what I had done in calming a situation that could have been more serious.

The point is that because I was a staff employee compared to these works employees, I had the obligation of acting on the company's behalf. This was all part of the inbuilt duty to our employer.

To return to a more personal issue, I have always had an interest in money and how it lubricates the economy and every-day life, whether in relation to wages, profit, pension schemes or even pocket money. I had a built-in natural affinity to express my views on how they all fit together. I became known for the use of my slim pocket diary which had facing pages covering one month. I used these built-in compartments to segregate my monthly cash spends – petrol, beer, etc. – and when there was a quibble about paying they used to say for God's sake Geoff, go to such-and-such a month in your book and pay up. I found this arrangement more practical than a wallet, which didn't have twelve sections.

I have always been interested in what appears to be a frequent debate on children's pocket money and the amount that should be paid at various ages. I recall how I personally dealt with the situation.

Just before Susan's fifth birthday I wanted to establish a fair system of allocating pocket money and avoid any misunderstanding. I established a procedure for implementing and applying such a policy. There would be an agreed minimum amount, irrespective of behaviour, and that would be unconditional. Additional money would be allocated on special occasions and after specific commitments. This provided the opportunity for our children to learn to save and budget, and perhaps to begin to learn the value of money. The rate I judged as fair was 1/6 pence (7.5p) at five years of age and £1 at 16.

At the time the pocket money was issued weekly because I was paid cash-in-hand weekly. My pay day was Thursday, therefore pocket money was allocated on a Thursday or Friday. This became a problem when my daughter's birthday was on a Friday, and she demanded the rate for the following week.

The systematic but simple plan I devised was:

- Before the first child is five years of age, establish a value of the amount to be paid at five and also at 16 or a later age.
- Obtain a piece of logarithmic/linear graph paper and enter the proposed amount at age 5 and at age 16 on the logarithmic scale, with the time in years on the linear scale.
- Draw a line between the two amounts at the respective ages and extrapolate the amount to be paid at each age inbetween.
- Review annually and allow for inflation or any other factor by drawing a line parallel to the previous one representing such an increase; this will automatically show the increase value at each age.
- Place the graph in a folder and relax (see Appendix N).

This system had the advantages of identifying the amount due; it covers any number of children, is inflation proof, transparent to all stake-holders and could be considered fair. It was not without its limitations; if you take the straight line literally, it can be argued that each week the child should have a marginal increase. If the system is just for guidance you don't need to do anything about that, but for more questioning children, especially when they are in their early teens, a stepped approach is advisable. If the graph is spread over too great a period it may be better to transfer the info to a new graph if the narrowing of the logarithmic lines may not provide the fine tuning that may be required.

Another of my monetary interests was pension schemes, especially the private sector schemes in addition to the schemes of the state. The two pension providers I had personal interest in were the Vickers Group Pension Scheme and the independent Foreman and Staff Mutual Benefit Society.

The Foreman and Staff Mutual Benefit Society scheme catered for foreman and staff employees and covered various options but mostly covered small pension contributions and limited amount of cover for sickness and redundancy. One of the restrictions was that you were not allowed to be a member of the scheme if you were a trade union member. The scheme aimed to encourage staff and foremen to be loyal to the company and, to encourage this, the company paid 50 per cent of the contributions. The total contribution was 10 shillings per week (50p), with the company paying 5 shillings (25p) and me 5 shillings.

I became a member on 27th November 1967, membership no. 133795. This was a good perk for staff employees and precluded the shop-floor workers because they were not at that time classed as staff and were predominately trade union members There was a "closed shop" operation in force, whereby you couldn't be employed as a works employee without been a member of the respective trade union.

In the mid-sixties, union membership was strong and staff unions were being formed and amalgamated. In 1969 Clive Jenkins, the General Secretary of the ASTMS (Union Association of Scientific, Technical and Managerial Staff) put a private members' bill through parliament to have clause (7) of the Foreman and Staff Mutual Benefit Society removed. He was successful, thus opening up membership to all staff employees. To this end I encouraged many of the NDT department members to join the Foreman and Staff Mutual Benefit Society. The scheme then altered its name to F & S Assurance, and it expanded rapidly and was eventually taken over by the Britannia Life

Insurance Company in the late 1990s.

The Vickers Group pension scheme was a contributory, salary-based scheme which in 1976 permitted members to be elected a trustee of the scheme. If a member could obtain 20 supporting signatures from other members of the scheme their name could be put forward to become a trustee of the scheme.

With my interests in pensions and my colleagues awareness of this I became some sort of authority on pensions. I soon obtained the 20 names required and duly sent off the application form in January 1977. One of the personnel officers at the time asked why I wanted to be involved with other people's problems. He had reservations from his own experience. I was perhaps rather naive about the more difficult aspects of being a trustee.

The selection was made by interview at the Vickers Group head office at Millbank Tower in London. This was one of the largest tower blocks in London and the interview room was very high up with an impressive view of London and the river Thames.

I travelled to the interview by train along with three or four other members from Barrow who also had appointments for an interview. I didn't know any of them personally but one of the first questions they asked me was which union did I represent, and I said none, that I was going as an individual. They were all there to represent trade unions and most held senior positions within the local branches of the unions. They had been elected on their union's behalf, rather than as individuals.

The union representation became apparent in the interview, where the panel consisted of senior managers, directors of the Vickers group, and national officers of Trade Unions.

I was not intimidated by the presence of such a distinguished panel and they tested me on my knowledge of the pension schemes and enquired whether I would be able to talk to up to 300 people about the scheme and answer any questions. I said yes. Then more specific questions were asked, and I remember the crucial ones from the APEX Association of Professional, Executive, Clerical and Computer Staff General Secretary, Keith Standring. He asked two questions. Firstly, which papers did I read? I said, *The Daily Mail* and *The Telegraph*. Then

109

he asked what were my views of investing pension-fund money in South Africa. This appeared to be a loaded question. I answered that as a trustee I have the duty to obtain the best return on the money invested. This may not have been the answer he would have liked!

From my journey down on the train and the specific questions asked it became apparent to me that there was an undercurrent of union involvement in the control of pension fund money. Over the years the unions had obtained a strong bargaining position for what was to happen on the shop floor, and now they were seeking a bigger influence on how and where money was to be invested. They would have a bigger say, not only on industrial production, services and labour, but on the finance that underpinned it.

I was unsuccessful but the interviewing and questioning was an experience and talking about finance at a relatively high level gave me a broader base for economic thought.

Early Holidays

On the 12th November 1972 we took our first family holiday abroad. I was not unduly bothered about foreign holidays but Tony Slone, my work colleague, who incidentally was the first person I knew who made use of a plastic card for drawing money out of what we call a hole in the wall, brought in some brochures to work and one lunch time I was browsing and saw a holiday to Tunisia. Doreen and I talked it over and we decided to go for it and within 48 hours I had booked the holiday this was one of my more impulsive buys. The holiday cost £120, £40 each for adults and £20 each for two children one aged seven the other five. The holiday was for a week in the Hammamet Hotel in Hammamet. Prior to the flight from Manchester we stayed in the Excelsior Hotel at Manchester airport the evening before departure. It was a most enjoyable holiday and the children enjoyed the sun and sand and the bargaining with the locals. One little boy asked us on the beach did we know Winston Churchill and we said yes; Do you know Georgie Best we said yes; Can I have some money we said no, and he immediately turned away and said you capitalist English pigs.

In July/August 1976 we arranged another family holiday, not quite abroad, but in Scotland. This was at a farm just east of Stirling at East Gogar where we rented a bungalow. We had arranged to have the use of the bungalow for a week. It was a detached bungalow in the ground adjacent to the farm house situated just off the A917 road between Stirling and Tullibody. It was surrounded by acres of flat, arable land and had as a backdrop the Ochil hills in a most beautiful setting. We made the journey in our white Austin Maxi, registration number REO 50L. On the journey there just near Lesmahagow (A74) the radiator hose burst and we pulled into a lay-by adjacent to a vehicle which had stopped for refreshment and by chance it was Alan Steel, an "ossick lad" who used to live in Great Urswick and was also holidaying in Scotland with his family and friends.

The farm was owned by Jim Snowie and his wife Sheila. They had four boys. The eldest, Malcolm was about 17, Alister was 13, Gordon 11 and Euan 8. They were all very boisterous and full of devilment and our children, Susan (12) and David (10) fitted in well.

Our hosts involved us in some farming activities including collecting hay, but our son David was extremely allergic to the hay pollen and his face swelled up until his eyes shut completely. Another of their boys' activities involved keeping the "Tullibodies" – youths from Tullibody, the next village – from raiding their vegetable crop. This was carried out from an old battered caravan strategically placed in the field and turns were taking in manning this post.

After the hay had been baled the bales were stacked and many were immediately transported in their own vehicle to hill farms in and around Killin.

After we had loaded the truck full of bales Jim and his son Malcolm invited me to go along with them to deliver the hay to a farm near Killin just north east of Callander. They told me that at that farm was a shepherd who had exceptionally curly-toed boots that curved in a half moon shape. Eventually they persuaded me to go with them at least to see the shepherd and his boots.

Off we set through Callander, the young lads wolf whistling and gesticulating to all the young girls on the way through. On the return journey we had fish and chips in Callander.

We arrived at the farm up a very narrow twisting road that would

111

just permit the lorry to pass.

As we were unloading the hay the shepherd started talking about "weshing sheep" and I knew this as a Cumbrian expression for washing sheep, usually by dipping them into a trough in the ground containing sheep dip or disinfectant. So I asked him where he came from and he said a place I wouldn't know in the English Lake District called Canny Hill just outside Newby Bridge near Windermere, and I could tell him I lived only about 6 miles from there.

Apparently he had been a shepherd near Thirlmere in the Lakes and had later taken his current job in Scotland. And yes, he did have long, curly-toed boots and they were made by George Redhead a boot supplier in Greenodd and were the type of hob-nailed boot made especially for shepherds that Doreen's uncles used when walking on Coniston Old Man and the other Coniston fells when herding and checking their sheep.

We enjoyed the holiday so much we booked to return the following year but on booking learnt from Mrs Snowie that her husband had died but that we were still welcome. Our friends from Ulverston, Vickie and John Leadbeater, came to join us that time, but they made use of the tents they brought with them and slept in the grounds of the farm.

We were accepted as part of the Snowie family and were invited to join them at their caravan at a caravan site on the shores of Loch Earn.

What so impressed me was the way Mrs Snowie and her four sons were coping with the farm after her husband's death. The sons were a bit of a handful but were also very supportive of her.

It was with great pleasure that much later my daughter sent me an article from the *Sunday Times* titled "Profit Track" and dated 13th April 2003 which listed Britain's 100 fastest growing firms and and Snowie Holdings, which was run by Mrs Snowie and her four sons was the 15th fastest growing firm in measured profit. They had diversified into waste management and had grown profits from £1.3m in 1998 to £8m in 2001 and the family were 84th in the *Times'* Rich List of 2004, having accrued a wealth of £33m.

It was soon after this that my mother died. She died at home in

September 1976, aged 74. She died peacefully in the end after suffering several years from a type of leukaemia. She passed away in the same serene way she had conducted her life, never causing a big fuss and in a reserved and dignified manner.

A year later, in the summer of 1977, we celebrated Queen Elizabeth II's Silver Jubilee. We had a street party and Doreen laid out a huge spread that covered our front and rear gardens with tables, and bench seats in the garage for the older persons. She and our neighbours did the celebrations proud.

By that time I had experience working in a technical service department which involved working with different skilled and unskilled personnel on a very wide basis of engineering and shipbuilding products. I had also become an authority on industrial radiography and my experience and understanding were often sought by designers, estimators, production planners and health and safety officers. I was now willing to take promotion to management grade if the opportunity arose.

CHAPTER FIVE

1980–1994
Aged 40–56 Years
Family Man and Manager

"The buzzer could be heard for miles around"

On the 1ˢᵗ April 1978 I was appointed Deputy Head of the Non-Destructive Testing Department. This appointment was a monthly staff position and increased my status within the company. Up until then I had been weekly paid, receiving my wages weekly, in cash, and receiving overtime payment at enhanced rates.

My new salary was based on the extra responsibility I had and the additional small factor of the extra hours I would be expected to do, but this was only a nominal amount and no way reflected the total loss of earning potential of overtime that I was relinquishing. The new salary would cover the general amount of overtime I was expected to cover. The new salary was calculated on the management grades which allowed for an annual increase for four years plus an element of merit money. So what I would enjoy was a higher basic salary and the potential to rise up the management pay structure. Although retirement was some time off for me the fact I had a higher basic salary had an impact on the amount of personal pension I would receive, being based as it was on years of service multiplied by pensionable pay, and these calculations were based on basic pay excluding payment for overtime or allowances.

The other big factor in the pension scheme was that your years of service included *all* your years as a staff employee, and not from 21 years of age when you were eligible to join and start contributing to the scheme. The fact that I started in a staff position at the age of 16 meant my pensionable years of service started from a relatively young age. This had a big influence later on when I was deciding on whether to take voluntary redundancy and was one of the factors in the final decision I made.

Going from a position of weekly pay with overtime payments to monthly pay and no payment for overtime gave me the incentive to manage my time more effectively. The thinking changed from maximising your hours paid to optimising the hours worked for a fixed salary. This meant more planning, delegation and time management. Also, the change from being weekly paid meant you had to work for up to four weeks without receiving any money because the monthly salary was paid into your bank account in arrears. This forced me to sit down and prepare a family budget based on monthly income and outgoings. This discipline has carried on and I still prepare an annual budget for guidance.

The budget preparation brought to my attention the smaller daily items on which money was spent which had a bigger impact on our annual expenditure than I thought, and if cost-cutting was to take place in the initial few months to get used to a fixed monthly income it was the small items purchased frequently, such as newspapers, magazines and incidentals that needed attention rather than annual larger fixed costs.

Doreen had become interested in taking some form of employment. She had spent some time in the local Croftland's primary school providing voluntary help with cooking for the small children but she spotted an advert in the *NW Evening Mail* for an assistant cook at High Carley Hospital which was about a mile from where we lived. The job involved 20 hours per week, from 9.00 am until 3.00 pm on weekdays, which was ideal for Doreen to fit in with the children's school day. Susan was then 14 and David 12.

She had never been for an interview in her life and was terrified, but was offered the job on 3rd September 1979. She still maintains this was one of the best things that had happened to her. It gave her some independence from me and family domestic life because up until then she had depended on other people for cash and personal spending money. Her tenacity for hard work and exceptional cooking abilities assured her position and within a short time she was promoted to a cook. Her cooking and entertaining skills were never in doubt and she brought to the job standards that were above and beyond the call of duty. These were standards which she insisted on, no matter at what level the cooking; even the small snacks at home involve a tablecloth, cutlery in the right position, and a general importance in presentation and pride.

Part of my own on-going responsibilities at work was to maintain and build on my knowledge and attributes. It was no longer guaranteed or acceptable that qualifications and skills obtained earlier would last you for life and you had to show you were keeping up-to-date with legislation and new methods of technology. This was the beginning of the Continuing Professional Development (CPD) ethic that was being introduced through personnel departments in go-ahead companies.

I had already attended a week's course at the National Radiological Protection Board's premises at the Cookridge Hospital facilities in Leeds in February 1978. This was for people to become classified as a person competent of applying the Ionising Radiation Regulations of 1969 which were so important given the large number of x-ray machines and radioactive isotopes we used in industrial radiography. It also included the safe storage and transportation of radioactive material.

One of the more incidental but disturbing events on the course was that if it was raining we would walk through the hospital buildings to the dining facilities and I witnessed the suffering of young children who were being treated for cancer. It is ironic that the ionising radiation we used for the inspection and analysis of materials can cause cancer by over-exposure, but if the radiation is controlled and focussed it can go a long way to curing the illness. I subsequently attended their 3-day radiation protection course for Radiation Protection Supervisors which had become a requirement under the 1985 Ionising Radiation Regulations.

In June 1982 as part of my interest in Industrial Radiography I enrolled to take a Diploma in Non-Destructive Testing. The Diploma was being introduced by the British Institute of Non-Destructive Testing and was intended to serve as a top-up qualification for those with managerial or potential managerial status in industry and who already held academic engineering or science qualifications.

Of the 23 candidates who took the examination only five were awarded the Diploma. The others did not come up to the expectation of the Diploma. It needed people with a broad knowledge and experience, and some of these who were only used to specialised aspects of Non-Destructive Testing found the syllabus too broad. The Institute then withdrew the Diploma course realising the catchment would be very low and not sustainable on an annual basis.

However my success in obtaining this Diploma gave me personal satisfaction from the private study I did and from taking on an independent small project.

In April 1984 my work duty was extended to encompass a satellite department which covered welding and fabrication inspection and was known as the Fabrication Quality Control Department. This involved about 14 personnel including welding and fabrication inspectors, and procedures for welding process control.

To help me in this appointment (in November 1984), I attended a course at the Cranfield Institute of Technology in Bedford. This course covered all aspects of Quality Assurance of weld and welded constructions. The course tutor was Mr John H. Rogerson and I was impressed by how he conducted himself and how he imparted knowledge to the class. To me he was one of the top professionals in this field. Around the same time I attended a week-long course titled "Finance for Non-Financial Managers" which was of interest and complementary to my duties.

My position within the company allowed me to attend annual conferences and exhibitions held by such organisations as the British Institute of Non-Destructive Testing in various parts of the UK, this enabled me to meet like-minded and work-related people and to update myself on aspects of NDT and Quality Assurance. I was of the opinion these were important events for gaining and passing on knowledge which offered good lectures on relevant topics which were supplemented by printed sheets and information documents if you didn't retain all the facts during the lectures. I also attended frequent events organised through the local professional institutes in engineering, management and other related topics. These all helped to gain a broad-based approach to problems which was preferable to dealing with issues in isolation. Many of the professional institutes allocated points for attending these events that were totalled up over a period of five years as evidence of a continuing professional development.

In 1984 I was invited to use the company's management dining room facilities. These facilities were for invited managers only and enabled production and technical managers to socialise who would otherwise, because of the size of the company, never make direct contact. It was a useful venue for discussion and communication which was not accessible during the working day. To this effect the company provided these meals for free, although later there was a deduction made from our salaries as a contribution to the subsidised meals. The dining room had waiter service, a choice of drinks and a three-course meal. The main management dining room was above the main shipbuilding works offices in Bridge Approach and adjacent to the general management dining room was the directors' dining room. Vickers provided other excellent canteen facilities to cater for works and staff personnel located in various positions within the works. These meals were of top quality and subsidised by the company.

One of the less onerous duties I had to perform as a function of middle management relating to production was to perform gate duty at noon and finishing time. The work force was permitted 5–10 minutes at the end of each shift to wash their hands and prepare for home. What happened as time went on was that the 10 minutes became 15 minutes. Fifty to a hundred employees would then gather around the exit doors of the various workshops and make their way to the gate that was nearest their place of work. To ensure compliance with this timekeeping discipline it became management policy for a pair of managers to be present at the exit areas on a rota system usually involving one week every three months.

It could be a nerve-wracking experience when a few hundred like-minded workman gradually formed a semicircle around the office near the gate. The indicator for the end of a shift was a buzzer that blew five minutes before the official finishing time followed by the final one at 12 noon and 4.30 pm. This buzzer could be heard for miles around, and also served the purpose of making the workforce aware it was five minutes to their starting time. Workman who failed to check in before the final buzzer were "quartered", that is they lost 15 minutes pay and if they were even later they would have to report to the foreman before being permitted to work. At finishing time it only took one person to provide an imitation sound of the buzzer and there would be an almighty rush which once started could not be controlled.

The secret I found was to maintain eye contact with the ones at the front of the crowd, which was sometimes difficult because sometimes the manager you were paired with would chatter, saying sorry I am late Geoff, or something, and once you lost direct eye contact with them they took that as the signal to make a break.

It was always a difficult duty, perhaps better in summer but in winter in the rain and cold it wasn't enjoyable.

Asbestos and Noise Pollution

A lot of my working environment has been in areas of noise and asbestos. The noise came from the continuous background sound of industrial machinery and pneumatic chipping hammers in the area I worked, which were used mainly to cut and shape metal as well as to remove any defective material on castings and welds.

The casting's defective areas were located by taking a tracing from the radiograph and applying it to the surface of the defective component. If this was a relatively thick-walled casting an x-ray technique was applied to ascertain the precise location of the defect through the wall in order to avoid the unnecessary removal of metal which had to be made good by welding. With the castings in the radiographic facility it was easier to set up an area within the department to cut and re-weld the defective areas. The result of this removal of localised areas of metal left the casting with surface dimples and irregular holes and, because of the various alloy constituents and previous heat treatment, when light was projected onto them they created a very colourful display and one project manager got disciplined when he described, in a report on the department, that the effect was as colourful as an autumn scene. This was not considered suitable for a technical report. Sometimes the defective areas had to be checked before welding to make sure the defects were removed.

Although most of the casting were positioned on sand bags and insulated booths to reduce the resonance and noise, at times the sound level of this metal-chipping process was in the region of 90–112 decibels. This was a noise you got used to but eventually it had a detrimental effect on my hearing. Industrial deafness became an issue in the regulation of industrial injury and health and safety. I was given the option, along with many others, in 1983, to go for a hearing test. This legal-aid arrangement was done through the management union SAIMA (Shipbuilding and Allied Industries Management Association) which later become part of the Engineers' and Management Association and they arranged for me to attend tests at North Lonsdale Hospital audio facilities. The test concluded that I had lost hearing to a certain frequency, and I was financially compensated accordingly in May 1983 with £715. This was a final settlement and no further claim could be made. For my hearing damage this was quite a high amount of compensation. The manual union members, although successful in their claims, were not paid out as much. This may have been due to the influence of the management union who obtained specialists in this field.

Another aspect of the working environment was the constant proximity to the asbestos lagging that was used to cover the steam pipes and nuclear reactor coolant pipes to reduce the loss of heat. I was not involved with the lagging process when it was initially installed, but part of re-inspection of welds in service meant the lagging had to be removed to obtain access to the welds. I was usually in the area when this lagging was being removed and the dry/wet fibres filled the air in these confined spaces. A similar test to the one for noise pollution was carried out on the people who had been exposed to asbestos who all had their lungs screened. The effects of asbestos injury may not become noticeable for up to 50 years after exposure, and some of my colleagues died from this or are still suffering from the consequences. A free assessment examination was set up using radiography CT to see if we had symptoms in our lungs of inhaling asbestos dust. An indicator of asbestos-related disease is the presence of pleural plaques. Fortunately in 2003 when I had the scan I was informed that I had no sign of pleural plaques in the lungs. This was a great relief for I felt I had a very high chance considering the environment I had worked in. However I registered with the company that I had been exposed to asbestos giving the relevant details of place and time.

Big Strike about Fixed Holidays

In the 1970s as part of the company's wage and salary negotiations it was in the interest of the company and its employees that all the employees were a member of a trade union or management association so the company could deal with groups and sections of the employee structure rather than individuals. We were encouraged or given the opportunity to join. I joined SAIMA, later part division of the Engineering Managers' Association. SAIMA was registered as a trade union for all managers and allied industries.

One of the advantages of membership of the union was it would represent you in any legal employment-related problem. Although it was not necessarily a militant group by the nature of its membership the union would back you if you were to take industrial action as a group. Of all the years I worked for the company I never took strike action. Although I may have sympathised with colleagues' complaints I was always in a position where it was up to my personal decision.

At the time of my working life industrial disputes were quite common, either involving sections of the workforce or the whole company. These disputes varied in content from work-to-rule, go slow, overtime ban or strike action, lasting from a few hours to days or sometimes even months. Most of the disputes were over who does what when some of the tradesmen's work overlapped, especially in the pipe work where different trades worked with different pipe material – the plumbers with lead, the coppersmiths with copper and the fitters with steel – and when welding was performed on all these the fitting up and preparation for welding caused job demarcation problems.

One of the major industrial disputes in the shipyard was in June

1988 when 13,000 employees walked out because the company insisted on going back to a fixed fortnight's annual leave with only the remaining holiday entitlement still flexible. The company had previously allowed holidays to be completely flexible. However they argued that this greater degree of flexibility was making the company's production unmanageable and they eventually got their way. This dispute wasn't settled until late summer.

One of the aspects of this massive walkout was that the company had still to maintain its security cover, fire service cover, and aspect of health and safety regardless. To provide this minimum amount of cover production management were called on to to cover in a monitoring/surveillance role and any breach was reported to security, the fire service or health and safety. This was done on a three-shift system of 12 hours, 3 days on 3 days off.

I was in the team that operated from the shipbuilding welding management offices. We had to patrol the perimeter which included the Walney channel frontage and the associated workshop for fire, health and safety, and security aspects.

This was a thankless job but we were getting our salary so we couldn't complain. Walking about in the empty workshops in the dark with a torch was a weird experience.

Other than exposure to general noise, asbestos and background radiation I was always privileged with good health and maintained a steady natural state of fitness but in April 1982 I underwent a hernia operation on my right-hand side lower abdomen. I think this may have originated in 1978 when I converted the integral garage to my house to a bedroom and constructed a garage behind and to the side of my house. I assisted the plasterer in mixing the plaster in a galvanised bath and the sideways paddling movement of the stodgy plaster over-strained the muscles I didn't normally use. This area started niggling me till eventually I had to have it seen to.

The operation took place in the North Lonsdale Hospital, St Georges Square, Barrow-in–Furness, and the operation was a success but the hospital environment struck me as barbaric, so I was glad to be transferred after a few days to High Carley which is set in nice surroundings and where I enjoyed my stay. I was off work for six weeks because I wasn't allowed to drive and I needed to recover from the after-effects of the anaesthetic and to regain the use of my muscles before I was fit again to work.

One of my disappointments was being in hospital on the day of the Rugby League cup final at Wembley Stadium as I had promised I would take my son David to the game. I have never been able to readdress this promise.

On 31st March 1984 my father died in Ulverston hospital after having to leave his home at Bank End Terrace a few months earlier after a slight seizure. Although this was expected, it was a loss to me. When he was at home in Urswick before going into hospital I visited every day. This was never a bind or chore for me as I got great satisfaction in providing this service. One week prior to my father's death Doreen's mother died from what started off as a slight stroke.

In the meantime my family were growing up. David left school at 16 in September 1983 to take up an apprenticeship in welding with Vickers Ltd and Susan went on to study for a degree in food marketing sciences at Sheffield City Polytechnic, Pond Street, Sheffield. David no longer wanted anything to do with further academic study and was happy in establishing a trade and earning his way in life. Susan on the other hand was more ambitious and always set out goals she wanted to fulfil and the course at Sheffield was a sandwich course which combined theoretical study with practical work placements and was one she had selected from several options.

Both Susan and David passed their driving test on the first attempt and this was thanks to their instructor, Mr Holme, who charged £6.50 hour. On one of his driving lessons with Mr Holmes in November 1985, David was involved in an accident, which was not his fault, when a car ran into the back of them.

Susan and David learned to drive in my Austin Maxi 1750 and when Susan had finished her driving instruction I had to have a replacement gear box fitted. Not her fault, it was just the general wear and tear, with a few helps on its way.

On taking the car to replace the gearbox at the garage in Barrow-in-Furness the lad at the reception took all the details and duly ordered the new gearbox and the car was left in the hands of the garage. A few days after fitting the replacement gearbox I noticed my milometer on the car registered my mileage to work as 5.8 miles when normally it was 8 and I couldn't understand this. So I queried it with the garage and what had happened was they had ordered a 1750 *Allegro* gear box instead of a 1750 *Maxi*. Although the physical size and bolting arrangements were the same, the gear ratio was different and the mileage difference was in direct relationship with the gear ratio. Not only was it measuring the miles travelled incorrectly, the speedo-meter reading on it was incorrect too and I was actually travelling faster than what it registered. This could have been quite significant in a speeding offence and would have probably gone unnoticed if I had been used to recording my mileage. I think the young lad got disciplined but it was only the difference in serial number he logged that caused the problem, although that should have been spotted before fitting!

Susan's time at Sheffield meant Doreen and I paid numerous visits there and for her first term (October 1983) she was in lodgings, organised through the polytechnic, at 17B Barnabus Road, Sheffield. This accommodation was basic and the family she moved in with were a husband and wife who were separated and they had a small child for whom Susan acted as a social worker and carer on numerous occasions. This was not a problem to her because she had a natural ability to cope with such a situation.

A lot of time was spent in taking Susan down to Kent where she did her work placement in The Apple and Pear Corporation office at Maidstone and also at a "Spotty Dick" factory in the area. One plus side to this was Susan always kept us involved and we saw parts of the country which we wouldn't normally have done.

David's apprenticeship was more orderly and he remained at home until moving to Dalton-in-Furness (in September 1987) where he had bought a 3-bedroom terraced house in Fell Croft, Dalton-in-Furness for £26,400 and moved in with his partner Vanessa, eventually marrying on 22nd December 1990. The wedding was overshadowed by the sudden death of Eileen, Doreen's brother's wife. She had gone into hospital a few days before the wedding and actually died on 21st December.

All the plans were in place for the wedding and we went ahead as near normal as possible. One of the features of the wedding was that Vanessa the bride wore a red dress and the bridesmaids wore white dresses. The parish church at Ulverston had been decked for Christmas in greenery and red decorations and the ceremony blended in well with the setting.

My managerial work duties now included overseeing a workforce of about 20 personnel consisting of supervisors, senior technicians, technicians, inspectors, clerical and ancillary workers, and the respective control of the equipment and facilities they used. Great emphasis had to be placed on health-and-safety and training, which were very stringent, especially when working with ionising radiation, not just for them but for other employees and, at times, the general public.

The company had good operating instructions and procedures, which were been continually updated.

Training, especially on-the-job training, had to be continually reviewed and implemented because there were always the new recruits to be trained and older ones kept up-to-date with the demands from new customers regarding qualifications and competency of personnel.

Another one of my duties was the departmental budgets for overheads, equipment and consumable items. I was constantly involved with the purchase-and-accounts department for the execution of this duty. The consumable items were a big factor because it included radiographic film, and the departmental budget for film alone at one time was around £100,000. Estimating was also an important responsibility. Although the company had large estimating departments which covered the pricing of general engineering items, they had to rely on people like myself for specialised services which only could be costed by people directly involved with the service and I built up a very good working relationship with the estimating, purchasing and accounts department.

The department was frequently asked to provide a small service for local industries that needed NDT services and who were not in a position to provide it for themselves, mainly because of the initial cost including the expense of trained personnel who would be required for only a short time. The company agreed we could help local companies, and the enquiries would come in and I would then have to discuss with the estimators and accounts departments how we would fulfil this service, bearing in mind that we were a very busy department and all the manpower was usually fully utilised.

However, we would come up with a pricing policy which did not include the full engineering company's overheads which were in the region of 300 per cent to cover all the costly machinery and facilities that would be engaged with their sophisticated engineering products. This only formed a minute percentage of our resources, but the introduction to the commercial aspect of the process with me being involved directly in taking the work on, in pricing and invoicing, improved my business approach further.

Even so, with the amount of radiography the department had to cover it could not cope and relied upon sub-contractors to do some NDT work and associated rectification work by welding. This was to do chiefly with the non-ferrous casting produced by our own foundry for the nuclear submarine programme and they consisted of several hundreds, from small handleable ones to the ones that required special handling equipment, and those that required the use of a 10-ton crane. The allocation for the radiography and subsequent work was part of my duty. This also included receiving them back and checking the subsequent invoice to verify the work carried out to allow the accounts department to approve payment.

This gave me an introduction to the operation of small businesses and medium-sized service companies, which I had to visit on many occasions to assess progress and oversee radiographs and inspection reports.

My other responsibility involved interviewing potential new recruits, discipline procedures and staff appraisals. The staff appraisals were an annual event for the people who were directly responsible to me. Periodically there was a not unlike process carried out for the selection for redundancy which was a form of individual appraisal, but without the personal contact.

For these appraisals to be carried out successfully, specific skills and application were required, and over the years it was a task I grew to feel comfortable managing, even in sometimes stressful circumstances.

Over the years I had had experience of working and communicating with a very wide range of individuals from those with low skills to the fully professional and academics.

When it came to the staff appraisal some individuals were wary of it, thinking it was a time when superiors could belittle or reprimand their subordinates, and that it was used for merit payment purposes only. This was far from the truth if the procedure was adopted and carried out by empathising with the individual; it became a very meaningful exercise and brought out a lot of advantages for the appraiser and those being appraised.

At the end of the appraisal interview the individual should feel reassured that their views and aspirations were listened to and a programme of training or other responsibilities granted that would make them more involved and feel more part of the department.

Some of these appraisals highlighted aspects of the individual that the appraiser or the company were not aware of. The capabilities and potential of some people sometimes lay dormant, in most cases due to a lack of confidence or the fear of putting themselves forward to bring matters up.

I was also subject to annual staff appraisals myself which I felt was both beneficial to me and the company. They highlighted my weaknesses and built on my strengths and gave a direction for the department and myself for the forthcoming year.

The procedure for selection for redundancy had to be adhered to strictly and fairly; if not, the company could be liable for a claim of unfair dismissal. On occasions I was involved with having to address this necessary but unfortunate procedure.

The selection criteria were spelt out in fine detail and they covered individuals, groups of workers, or whole sections depending on the company's specific requirements regarding redundancy in the target area. Redundancy means the position or job is redundant, not the individual. Some individuals were moved to other departments which were not in a redundancy situation. The selection and appraisal criteria included such aspects as knowledge of the job, skill range, job interest, target achievement, self-reliance, team work, conduct, length of service; all these categories had a weighting and a point system of 1 to 7 and the individual was assessed using these categories.

The points allocated and the weighting were multiplied together to provide a total score for each individual in the respective groups. However it was not automatic that the one with the lowest score had to go because there was an appeal procedure and the scores could be challenged. Also if an individual scored low and had some particular skill and knowledge that the company required they could be retained.

All the scores were evaluated and checked by the personnel department and the individuals concerned were informed that they were been considered for compulsory redundancy. Prior to the redundancy selection procedure the company offered volunteers for redundancy to come forward and register their intent. This was ideal for people wanting to leave or who were near retirement and when redundancy would suit their particular circumstances. The volunteers were sometimes at a slight disadvantage over the compulsory redundancies in the way they were treated regarding social benefits, including mortgage repayments. If you volunteered you were not immediately entitled to these.

On one occasion I was approached by a technician who asked me to make him redundant rather than he do so voluntarily. The downside to this was that in a compulsory redundancy situation the selection procedure may have excluded him because of his attributes and worth to the company on the basis of the selection criteria. He said he wouldn't use this against the company later on but a few weeks after the event he may have changed his mind and you could never take that chance. A claim for unfair dismissal could be embarrassing and costly.

Other aspects of getting it wrong could result in the company being taken to an Industrial Tribunal. I became involved in the early stages of an Industrial Tribunal situation in 1984 which concerned one of my department staff who was spending too much time away from the company on local and county council business.

This was at the time when new labour laws permitted local and county councillors a reasonable time off in company time to carry out their duties and may have been set up as a test case to define what is reasonable. This particular individual was a foreman in a small section of 14 inspectors. He was spending up to three days a week on council business and although he thought he had the right, the company decided that this amount of time away from work was unreasonable.

He carried putting requests in to me for time off to attend the council meetings. Each request had on the top "without prejudice" (he had taken advice). I had to put him on the first stage of a disciplinary warning and subsequently he went to the second stage and prior to the third stage he was warned that the outcome could result in his losing his job. He came the third time for time off and I informed him of that consequence, which he fully understood.

He was quite confident he was on good ground and at the time he was backed up by the local MP for Barrow-in-Furness and government employment minister, the Right Honourable Albert Booth. The foreman in question told me he was feeding his solicitor raw eggs, indicating he was getting him fighting fit.

After the third stage of discipline the three stages were then reviewed by the personnel department to decide what action should be taken. This was then taken to higher levels because personnel thought it could be a test case for what was considered reasonable under the law.

As a result he had to attend a tribunal and the company's case was upheld that he could only have one day per week to carry out his council duties and the case attracted a lot of local media and television coverage at the time (see *NW Evening Mail*, 24 January 1985). During and after the case there was no animosity towards me.

He left the company and continued with his council and county council involvement and became the Chairman of the Lake District National Park and was later awarded the OBE for his services in 2004. This was a man who had a passion for public service.

Of the people made redundant through my assessment no one ever complained or appealed against the decision. Redundancy is personal and can be life changing. The interviews were done on a one-to-one basis in a fair and objective manner. At the final interview of three there was a brief talk confirming the finality of the individual being made redundant.

I remember I had to make three out of four female clerical staff redundant and when it came to the final interview each was scheduled for three consecutive interview times. They came as a group so I asked them to come in one at a time which was the formal way because what you had to say to one may not be applicable to the other and vice versa. However they insisted on coming in together and I talked to them in a group discussion, and at the end they asked, "Where do we sign?" and they duly did so, and then they all went out with their shopping bags to carry out their domestic duties. It could have been a difficult situation but with trust and respect on each side the situation was finalised amicably.

I had my own experience of attending internal job interviews but one incident comes to mind when I had entered on my CV my interest in playing musical instruments. One person on the panel asked, "What do your family think of your musical talent?" I replied, "Put it this way, I went home one evening to find my wife had been stirring the Dulux gloss paint with my penny whistle." This caused amusement but it also showed my wife's initiative and practical thinking in finding a good implement that could stir paint efficiently. The penny whistle must have been stored in one of the drawers at hand when a stirrer was required.

One of my pastimes was to attend a group play-along involving folk and traditional music on Thursday evenings at the Manor Park public house in Oxen Park. I took along my penny whistle in my pocket and the landlord, Mr Oldham, played the guitar and he suggested that any person who showed interest and wanted to join the group were allowed to. The group could sometimes be as few as five but I have seen up to twelve people and more attending. Many of the individuals came from far afield; there was some from the Langdale valley who played violins. This was a very therapeutic evening and perhaps one of the reasons it came to an end for me was the introduction of the breathalyser test. Having the journey to make back from the venue I could not take the risk.

In the meantime I continued with my professional development, being expected to keep up to date with current thinking and knowledge. In 1989 I decided that although I was competent in aspects of Non-Destructive Testing, I felt my position within the company needed to be evaluated against an external benchmark and to be demonstrable and creditable.

I was aware of the American system for training and certification of personnel involved with NDT which provided both a company-based and an independent, nationally-based certification. The scheme has international recognition and could be adopted for any company providing it was operated within the guidelines of the scheme which has built-in flexibility for small or large companies irrespective of the product they are testing.

This scheme is controlled and organised through the American Society of Non-Destructive Testing (ASNT) and is based on three levels of competency: Level 1 for employees who could carry out work under supervision; Level 2 for those who could carry out inspection on their own and were capable of supervising level 1 and who would be expected to carry out inspection and assess the findings against the respective standard; and Level 3 for those expected to be capable of providing guidance and advice on technique suitability and overall training.

These levels are applied to the specific discipline in which approval is being sought. The main theme and fundamental requirement behind Level 1 and Level 2 training and certification is presented in a written document that lays out how a company trains and certifies its NDT staff in accordance with a Recommended Practice for Personnel Qualification in Non-destructive Testing. This written practice is a flexible document that could be tailor-made for any large or small company, although the basic requirements were applicable in all cases. This gives the flexibility for small, specialised companies to train staff on their own company products for what their clients required. Some type of training may be irrelevant or too specific for their company's products, thus allowing them to be trained and certified in the application of the inspection method that was relevant for what their company required to fulfil contractual obligations.

My particular interest was in the Level 3 category of examination and certification which included the main methods of NDT which my company was involved in. The Level 3 status was acknowledged as a level of competence and professional standing in applying, training and supervising NDT operations across the world.

Prior to taking the examinations at Level 3 you had to demonstrate you had had the years of experience and involvement in NDT at a fairly high level of responsibility and the necessary background to apply and promote the scheme.

I discussed this with my company who agreed to pay for the cost of the examinations. All the study was at my own expense and time. You could either attend the examination in America, which were held quite frequently or wait until the annual one was conducted in this country. The timing of the ones in this country allowed me time to study for the examination because most of it involved self-study, although I attended refresher courses, especially on how the ASNT scheme operated. This was at Lavender International training facilities at Penistone, South Yorkshire with whom I had built up a good relationship through the involvement of my NDT operators' training, especially with Jack Lavender, the founder of the company himself, his son Steve, Roger Hamlett and Gary Elliott who at the time was also taking the Level 3 examinations. In addition to technical competency, knowledge of the operation of the examination scheme was a mandatory part. This was important because a Level 3 could train and assess individuals against theses requirements. You also had to have a broad knowledge of manufacturing and fabrication methods and other disciplines of NDT you were not being specifically been examined for.

I took the examinations at Sandwell Technical College, Walsall, over two days. If you did not pass the basic examination, no matter how well you did in the individual method examination, you were failed.

These were broad-based examinations and no single written

examination could test your knowledge and understanding of all the parameters that were required.

Hence these examinations were all multi-choice. Some of the examinations were for 4 hours and others for 2 hours. You selected the disciplines that you were seeking approval in, but the basic examination paper which was mandatory included how the system operated and some basic knowledge of other disciplines you were not being examined on. I selected: Radiography, 4 hours; Magnetic particles, 2 hours; and Liquid Penetrant testing, 2 hours.

In the four-hour exams you were expected to answer 120 questions with the choice of five options to indicate the correct answer. This was not only about knowledge, it also tested your ability to resolve NDT situations in a short time as would would be expected in a working environment. You had to carry out calculations and decisions against the referenced specifications. The examination paper, including your name and registration number, was A4 size or American equivalent. You read the question from another pamphlet and were provided with supporting information regarding specification and extracts from various codes, indicating your answer by selecting the respective circle on the answer paper. This was a very efficient and effective way of testing if an individual was up to standard.

All the examination papers and reference documents were gathered up by the invigilators after the examination and duly placed in an envelope provided by and returned to America. The A4-size examination paper was then scanned through a computer and you were either provided with a pass or a fail. In border-line cases the supporting information and the notes you had made would be taken into consideration because sometimes if you can justify your answer you were given the benefit of the doubt. Sometimes question could have more than one meaning depending on the wording of the question, and if you explained the reasoning for your answer it could be counted as correct. It was more to do with reasoning and understanding rather than simply right or wrong.

Although these examinations were demanding, it was said that if you knew your subject well you should not have a problem in passing. I was successful in obtaining certification in all my three chosen subjects and the fact you passed the basic exam allowed you to take exams in other disciplines at a later date without taking the basic examination again. I took Ultrasonic the following year.

Having passed these examinations a certificate was awarded showing all the aspects of my approval. This was displayed in my office and at times when the company or the department was being audited, especially with regard to American contracts, it did away with a need to demonstrate you were competent. Just a glance at the certificate was enough for the auditors to ask the more searching questions knowing full well the background and status of the manager. This certificate wasn't mandatory but once in place it answered a lot of questions that may have been asked, although in some cases for specific work the company had to have a registered Level 3 in place. I recall one American auditor on been taking around the workplace audit remarked "I can find shite in a cuckoo clock".

Health Matter

From the age of 17 I underwent, through the company, regular blood tests. In the early days this was every three months and then it became part of an annual medical examination. This medical was a requirement to be compliant with the ionising radiations regulations for a classified worker who may potentially receive a pre-determined level of radiation from using ionising radiations as part of their work. The medical included height, weight, eyesight, and blood pressure checks as well as the blood test, followed by a final discussion with the works doctor or medical officer.

In September 1990, however, when attending my annual medical and finally reporting to a new woman company doctor for an overall review, she told me they were no longer carrying out the blood test because its value over the years had been reduced and it was measuring historical information after the event. The new regulations permitted this and the blood test would only be conducted on individuals who have been exposed to an abnormal level of radiation or individuals who have a good reason for one.

I said that I would like a blood test; she reeled back in her chair with her face taut and her eyes out of alignment. "And *why* do you want a blood test?" as she projected her voice towards me. I explained that I had had a regular blood test since I was 17 and my records would show this and it would be false economy to stop at this stage. I considered it relevant to me that there was a continuing record of my blood tests, bearing in mind most of the radiation I received was when I was relatively young and radiation-induced disease may not manifest itself for a number of years. She told me my exposure to radiation was no more than people who worked at the nuclear power station up the coast at Sellafield. I explained my exposure to radiation had been with me all my working life and in some cases when dealing with nuclear reactors in service inspections I was not just exposed to radiation but radioactivity.

"Well, Mr Elleray, in this case I will permit you to have one but in future that will not be the case." I said, "Thank you. Do I go and see Brenda as usual in the works pathological laboratory?" and she replied, "No, Brenda is no longer with us." "Oh," I remarked. I said she was the highlight of my medical. "You will get a common nurse like anybody else, Mr Elleray," she replied.

I thought this approach and attitude is one I wouldn't normally expect from a professional person. She must have been having an off day. She had a different attitude to the previous works' doctor who carried out this duty. One male doctor would ask simple searching questions such as "How's the teapot?" or "Do you know what they do with old razor blades?" and I said, "no," and he said, "they make engines out of them." He was a big steam-engine enthusiast.

A few days later I received a telephone call from the doctor to say would I arrange to come to the clinic to have another blood sample taken. I duly did so and when the results came back I had to go and see her. I was greeted with: "This is what happens when you have blood tests taken." I asked if there was a problem. She replied, "Put it this way; your blood is not the same as mine." I said, "I didn't ask that. Have I got a blood disorder or not?" She said there is a problem with your platelets. They were showing as being large and low in number. I would like you to attend the Furness General Hospital pathological laboratory for further tests."

On attending the laboratory they wanted to take about 15 samples of my blood and they had the needles and syringes lined up in a row on the bench adjacent to where I was sitting. This frightened me somewhat because I have always been squeamish in having needles put into me. I said to the nurse, "You may get the first two in but you won't get the rest." However as time has gone on they now only insert one needle and draw numerous amounts of blood into separate bottles which are removable from the needle, so the fear is no longer there.

After the samples were taken and analysed I had to attend an interview with Dr Macheta, the blood specialist. It was a cold day and I had a heavy anorak on. Dr Macheta's office was humid and had little fresh air. While he was explaining what the blood problem was in a voice that was monotone and hypnotic, I became dizzy and rather faint. I mentioned to him that I felt faint but it didn't register with him as he continued talking and in the end I had to be quite firm and say I didn't feel well. He said he had to examine me and took me into a room across the corridor where he asked me to lay on the bed. He was at my right side and I had raised my left leg to get onto the bed when I must have fainted and landed on the floor. The next thing I heard was "Take his jacket off!" I started to get up and someone said, "Stay there, don't move," and within minutes the cardiac arrest staff were looking down on me, clutching their probes, and nurses with fishnet tights were also kneeling over me and all I could see was thighs and fishnet tights. I thought I was in heaven.

This was all over in a matter of minutes and I was as right as rain. Although my blood pressure had gone down to 30 pulses per minute and rose quickly to 60. Apparently what had happened was that when I tried to get onto the bed I fainted and the tie around my neck was rather tight and on fainting it had put pressure on my neck resulting in me going blue. They thought I was having a heart attack and hence the cardiac arrest squad were sent for. Nobody could understand what the cardiac arrest unit was doing in the path lab. They took seven minutes to arrive, which had to be logged to make information available for their response time.

The blood test results confirmed my platelets were large and low and I was asked to attend every three months for a check. This eventually became an annual check and I still attend to this day. The fact remains that my platelets are still large and low but the variation is still within acceptable limits, but if further deterioration takes place action may be required.

I am very grateful to Furness General Hospital and especially to Dr Macheta. Dr Macheta is aware why I asked for these continuing checks to be continued and he is in agreement and understands the implications.

At the time I was suffering also from "tennis elbow", an inflammation of the tendons of the elbow caused by overuse of the forearm muscles in my left arm and was wondering how I could get my arm working normally without over-straining it. I decided that swimming could be the activity that could improve the situation.

I started visiting the swimming baths in Ulverston which is just down the road from me and I would potter about doing up to about six lengths with breaks in between. The swimming gradually improved and so did my arm mobility and ever since then I have attended the swimming baths on a regular basis. On average I attend the early morning swim programme at 7.30 am for about an hour once a week and now consistently do between 50 and 60 lengths.

Redundancy

In the early part of 1994 there was a further redundancy programme or what was euphemistically described as a "restructuring programme" by the company due to the Cold War pressure easing and the subsequent lack of shipbuilding and engineering orders including the nuclear submarine constructions. Once again as in previous restructuring programmes the company asked for volunteers. This programme offered an incentive package for those seeking redundancy, noticeably enhanced pension benefits and a lump sum payment. This appealed to me and was an opportunity worth considering.

The pension offer was you could take your pension at 50 years of age but you would lose 1% each you below 60. The fact I was 55¼ years old meant I would loose 4.75% of my entitlement. The fact was

I had 39 years service already and the maximum for full pension entitlement was 40. I would have to forfeit 1% of my pension for each year below the age of 60, which would leave me with 36 calculated years service. This offer was attractive to me, because at the time jobs were being downgraded and team leaders on lower salaries were being brought in. In the right circumstances it could work out with mutual benefit to me and the company. There could also be the potential risk over the next few years that the enhancement on offer may not be repeated. Also there was the uncertainty of whether the existing level of basic salary may be reduced – possible but improbable.

Deciding to take voluntary redundancy required some logical thinking and basic calculations of the facts available and allowance for the unforeseen.

My decision to proceed or whether to apply for voluntary redundancy went something like this:

At my age of 55 years and 3 months what would be my total expected earnings to 65 years of age? Nine years and three quarter times a year's salary.

Then deduct:
• National insurance at 8%
• Pension contributions at 6%
• Cost of travel to work

As against:
• The value of my pension
• Potential of further work income
• The interest on my lump sum investment
• The freedom to do other things

When all this was taken into consideration the difference between net income from working and net income from retirement was not great enough to be unmanageable, bearing in mind the freedom and flexibility I would gain.

Though I had the opportunity to apply for voluntary redundancy it wouldn't be automatically granted and I had 2–3 months to prepare for it and the last thing I wanted once I had in my mind to go was to be prevented from doing so, although this was unlikely it was a possibility for the company to say you can't be released. The company held the right to retain special skills or experience.

I made the decision I would take voluntary redundancy and the wheels were put in motion. The only thing that was unique to me and important to the company was my American ASNT Qualification which if considered of sufficient value to the company might deter them from letting me go. I brought this to the attention of my manager and directors to get assurance on this. I didn't want to set my goals on retiring and planning and then be prevented at the last minute.

My company pension was a final salary scheme but one of the critical factors that were brought into the calculation was that my pension payment was calculated on the previous year's salary and not the current one, which had only a week to run. But the company offer of the attractive redundancy package ended on the 31 March 1994 and if you worked the extra week for the additional year's pension you missed out on the attractive package. The decision was made and I never regretted it.

This was the time in my life when the mortgage was paid off, the children were away from home, but not quite entirely independent. Our first grandson, Dean, was born on the 31st May 1993. Doreen was working part-time and there was a sense that things were going to change. It was a decision I made but Doreen was rather sceptical, dreading the days I would be under her feet and dictating the household policy. I said, "Don't worry love, I won't be under your feet." Our daughter Susan had graduated from Sheffield Polytechnic in the summer of 1987 with a 2.1 in food marketing science and she started with her first job as a representative for the Milk Marketing Board in Essex, living in rented accommodation in Colchester. With the demise of the Milk Marketing Board she then got a position at the Head Office of the superstore Asda in Leeds, working under the direction of Archie Norman and Alan Leighton.

During the run-up to redundancy the company encouraged employees to attend courses on the support available, including pre-retirement courses. I had my own plans on how I would cope, including capitalising on my knowledge and experience, keeping active and, in the first instance, not turning down any offer of work or opportunities.

I finished full-time work on the 31st March 1994.

21a, b, c. *Me the musician, playing the accordian, piano and pennywhistle*

22. *Me with Urswick sports shield*　　　23. *Me with Ferguson tractor*

24. *Me in working boiler suit*　　　25. *Me with beard*

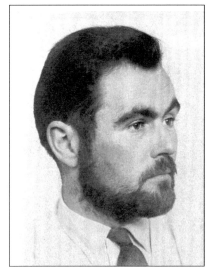

26. *Our wedding, 10 November 1962*

27, 28. *Outside Colton Church. Above left to right: Carole Phillipson, John Park, Enid (my sister), groom and bride, Walter Phillipson, Joan Harris, Marion Wood, Myras Casson; and centre, Jane Boyron*

29. *Above: loading hay at the Snowie's farm*

30. *Snowie's caravan, Loch Earn, Gordon Snowie, Susan, our daughter, David, our son, and Euan Snowie*

31. *Susan and David flying kites at the Snowie's farm*

32. *Me presenting Alisa Hampshire the ASNT, North Atlantic Section, Technician of the Year Award*

33. *Me and Gail (Helen Worth), from* Coronation Street, *at the Prince's Trust 25th Anniversary, Old Trafford, Manchester*

34. *Me and Doreen at the same event*

35. *Dad's 80th birthday. Back: Alan (brother-in-law), Susan (daughter), Helen (friend); Middle: Hazel (neice), David (son), Kathleen (cousin), Stephen (nephew), Enid (sister), Doreen (wife); Front l to r: (Aunty) Peggy, Dad, me*

36. *En route in Germany with Doreen and Mr and Mrs Bowyer*

37. *Bungalow, "Duneden", Dunnet Head, north of Scotland, 1967*

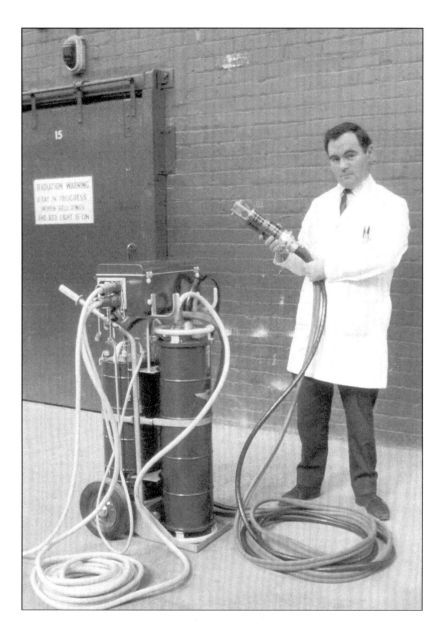

38. *At work, with an x-ray set, Non-Destructive Testing department*

CHAPTER SIX

1994–2003
Aged 56–65 Years

Semi-retirement, Self-employment,
The Prince's Trust, Business Counselling

"A natural progression"

After taking voluntary redundancy from Vickers and having a semi-retirement mindset in place I had to readjust the way I thought and what I was going to do. I was approaching 56 with 9 years until I received my state pension, but fortunately I was able to draw my company pension, which I had assessed as being adequate to survive on and still enjoy some spare cash that would provide for the replacement of household equipment and modest holidays.

Prior to taking redundancy my finances had to be evaluated and it was important to get my post-redundancy finances – investments and pensions – in place. Vickers provided the names of financial advisor companies. I selected Bowring Financial Services based in Manchester to provide me with a financial retirement plan and the chap I had personal dealings with was Wally Kulczyckia, Divisional Director, who liked to be known as just "Wally", a small Polish gentleman who provided me with a plan and forecast and gave the advice both in the written and verbal form which reassured my own thoughts.

The freedom and flexibility that was now available to me required some constraints putting in place so my life could be structured to eliminate the propensity to drift and fritter away opportunities. I was still interested in the NDT and Quality Assurance environment and wanted to continue using my knowledge and experience to help local companies who were involved with NDT and related projects. Because of the small number of local companies that required NDT services, scope was rather limited. However I had an open mind and the amount of involvement and the numbers of hours and travel I was prepared to put in would be small relative to a full-time job and would allow me to spend more time with my family and in leisure.

During my last few weeks at work there was a part-time course advertised in the local paper which was to be provided and organised by the Centre for Continuing Education, Training and Development (CETAD) of Lancaster University through their Charlotte Mason College at Ambleside. This course was a Training Consultancy Development Programme and funded through KONVER which was part of the European Social funds and Lancaster University.

The course was due to start on 11th April and finish on 4th November 1994, a thirty-week course organised at 18 hours per week so that claimants for state benefits would be still eligible without loosing any benefit. The course came under the administration and implementation of Kathy Joyce (Head), Julian Jordan (Programme Manager) and lecturers Chris Ogilvie, Jane O'Brian and Sue Nutter, all CETAD staff, and it involved three days a week but included outplacement work and time for private study. It gave an opportunity for people who, due to redundancy or personal requirements, needed direction. The course was flexible and adaptable to personal requirements.

I wasn't eligible for state unemployment benefits but I registered as unemployed to maintain my national insurance contributions of which I only required a few to fulfil my life-time requirement for a full state pension. I was prepared to make full use of what was on offer and what the course could do for me. Due to the fact I had been made redundant, under a scheme the government had put in position, as with other students I was eligible for a free place. If the funding had not been available the course fee would have been £2,500 so I was very grateful for having this amount of training free. Not only the training but the networking and opportunities that were available.

The course was held locally at the Trinity Enterprise Business Centre facilities in Barrow and we had access to student study facilities through Lancaster University. The course was designed to help, if you wished, to become an effective professional training consultant or a consultant in the field you were interested in, and included a personal development programme, training and development skills, accreditation, becoming a consultant, and business planning. The salient parts covered business training, counselling and self-employment. It enabled the trainee to work towards nationally recognised qualifications appropriate to their choice of specialisation and provided tutoring and advice on how to become a consultant. The course also provided study of the national vocational qualifications (NVQs) and how they fit into the national education structure. Whilst on the course you were encouraged to go in for some of the units of competence which represented aspects of performance that are large enough to be of value to an employer. An example was the D31 and D32 units, part of the full award of the Training and Development Level 3 standards to become an NVQ Assessor. This could be applicable to people who are not trainers but merely want to be qualified in those components. The standards for the NVQs are set by industry sectors through lead bodies and therefore can be structured to what industry requires. I managed to obtain units applicable to Level 4 "Training and Development" in identifying and prioritising training and development needs and organisational training.

The ground covered in the syllabus was ideal in helping me through the transition from working for an employer to becoming self-employed and allowed me to be able to offer a portfolio of services to different types of individuals and companies. In parallel with the course I was promoting myself as an NDT and Quality Consultant, helping local companies with specific issues and support, although in many instances I would not be able to fulfil all their needs. I would be a catalyst and contact to signpost them on the way ahead especially on aspects of quality control and assurance, technical aspects and training needs that were required both then and in the future. My initial contacts were with local engineering companies including St Andrew's Engineering, Scurrah Nassau, Tronic, Strand Engineering and other inspection service companies that needed verification/approval on certain NDT procedures. I was authorised to write and approve procedures through the American scheme of NDT (ASNT) and conduct training and invigilate for

NDT examinations. One of the companies I dealt with was Flaw Spec NDT Ltd, with contact made through Ken Hibberd who lived at Slackhead near Milnthorpe, and which operated service inspection companies in South Lancashire.

I wasn't seeking to be working 40 hours a week with a demanding schedule and earning lots of money, but hoped more for a fulfilling social activity as well as providing a contribution to my finances.

This consultancy course provided me with an induction and framework to remain active and part of society – a form of apprenticeship for semi and full retirement. An important factor for me was how to manage my time so that I would be able to do what I wanted when I wanted to, and to combine it with family life and holidays.

In 1993 at its inaugural meeting I had become a member of the North Atlantic Section of the American Society of Non-Destructive Testing, and subsequently, in 1998, I became a committee member. The members were chiefly from the industrial, manufacturing and aerospace industries of the United Kingdom but I was mainly involved around the midlands and the north of England.

The committee consisting of about 12 voluntary members who would meet every four to six months in various industrial premises or offices of companies that made use of Non-Destructive Testing, training providers and equipment suppliers who all had an inbuilt interest to promote the advantages of NDT to industry and beyond.

Sometimes I found it difficult to attend the meetings, especially those held in the south of the country. However, I regularly attended the meetings in Leeds, Manchester, Derby, and Rotherham. These meetings always involved the business side of the meeting but also included visits around the various factories, including Rolls Royce and Associates at Derby and BAE Systems at Warton where the meetings were held. I also attended the annual conferences and the first few were held at the American Embassy premises in London. This kept me current with any relevant information which I could pass onto local companies, and participating in the networking that was inherent in these meetings.

I served on the committee from 1998 for five years. My main role was as Education Director and one of my duties was to organise the

"Technician of the Year Award". This award went to a technician who had shown the good application and promotion of NDT to the benefit of the customer and the company. An applicant had to be nominated by their employer. The award was to promote recognition for individuals who very rarely got credit for the work they do and to help bring a feeling of involvement to parts of industry that sometimes become alienated. These technicians rarely receive any recognition and the award is based on an allocation of points against factors such as job related accomplishments, meetings attended, membership of NDT societies, project work and employer's references. These technicians are at the coalface where outstanding applications of NDT take place; so this award normally excludes senior technicians, supervisors and managers who are in a position of authority which brings its own recognition.

Soon after resigning from the committee I was awarded the J.D Lavender Lifetime Achievement Award from the North Atlantic Section of the American Society of Non-Destructive Testing. This was in recognition of my lifetime work in NDT. I received the award at the University of the West of England, Bristol, at their Annual Conference on 12th April 2006. I felt this to be a great honour and gave my working life a sense of completeness, having started off as an apprentice at 16 and receiving professional recognition from my peers when I was 68.

Princes Youth Business Trust (PYBT)

A few weeks after finishing work in the Spring of 1994, I was approached by the "Job Shop" which had been set up by Vickers to help people who had been made redundant in preparing CVs and to provide access to local and international job vacancies.

Janet Whittaker, the manager of the Job Shop at the time rang to ask me if I would be interested in doing work for the Prince's Youth Business Trust (see Appendix O). She had been asked by Vickers to approach ex-managers and enquire whether they had any interest in contributing, and said she didn't know much about the requirements or what the request involved but considered me a likely candidate and if I was interested she would send me more information.

Part of my philosophy at the time was to keep all my options open and not to turn down any potential opportunity. I said I would be interested and immediately went to the local library to find information on the structure and purpose of the Trust. Although I had heard about it I did not know the extent of its work and how it operated. Janet said I might not hear more for some time.

However, true to her word, on 6ᵗʰ February 1995 I received a letter from Janet asking me to provide a CV and offering the details for me to attend an interview at the Training School of Vickers. I attended the interview along with other ex-managers who had also been approached for the position. At this stage the outline of the job requirements and what was expected of the position were discussed. There was some degree of flexibility in what was expected to fulfil their requirements, which suited me.

Vickers, like many other companies, saw PYBT as part of their way of supporting the local area, and especially the young unemployed and disadvantaged young people of the district, and it participated a lot through its own apprentice training schemes, especially at times of large redundancy programmes which affected the apprentices.

They supported the PYBT mostly in kind and seconded a junior manager to the PYBT on a part-time basis. This was to support the Trust but also to give junior graduate managers broader experiences than they would normally obtain.

During 1994 the relationship between Vickers the secondee and the PYBT was reviewed. It was decided that instead of having an existing employee carrying out the duty they would support an ex-Vickers manager who may be interested in taking on the role and also pay a token fee to the Trust. Hence I was approached.

The interview panel consisted of Charlie Fairhurst, Vickers Personnel Officer; Alan Hurst, Manager PYBT Cumbria, seconded from British Nuclear Fuels Personnel Department; and Brian Hetherington from Vickers who was the incumbent part-time seconded person to the Trust.

I felt comfortable in the presence of the panel and had the satisfaction of knowing that there was no necessity for me to take the position and before committing myself it was up to me to find out what the post involved and up to them to decide whether I was the right person for the position. They were looking for somebody with a broad experience rather than a specialist and a person who was motivated and could empathise with young people.

I had just got back home from the interview when the telephone rang and it was Mr Fairhurst asking me if I would take the position. I was surprised by the promptness for I was expecting a letter in a few days. I was put on the spot. I said yes. He replied, "Everyone on the panel will be glad you have accepted," which gave me much confidence that I was the sort of person they were looking for.

Alan Hurst drew up a contract for my involvement which would make use of the skills I had and some that I would have to revise, such as the use of business plans, profit and loss, accounts, cash flow and the legal requirements of self-employment. I rose to the challenge and the experience gained provided me with a background that became invaluable in helping individuals to start up in business, or otherwise directing them down another route that was more suitable for them, and for me was to be a rewarding and happy relationship with the business scene in the Furness area and beyond.

I was expected to work the equivalent of 2 days per week with the hours to fit in with my other activities and I would receive a symbolic fee provided by Vickers to the PYBT for carrying out my duties. I was allocated a desk and office support facilities at the local enterprise agency, Furness Enterprise, at Trinity Enterprise Centre, Barrow-in-Furness.

This arrangement worked well. I had access to telephone, secretarial support, consulting room facilities, a computer and up-to-date information on the local business scene as well as contact with the movers and shakers of an enterprise culture. This arrangement was of mutual benefit to the PYBT and Furness Enterprise which had just been set up by the three Local Authorities with Harry Knowles as the Chief Executive. The aim of the organisation was to assist with the regeneration of the area after heavy local redundancies and was an example of a facility working together for a common purpose in serving all the people and companies seeking support in business.

As part of my PYBT activities I attended a 2-day induction course in London on how the Trust operated where I met up with some of the senior and secretarial staff at the head office. The same induction was also attended by Alan White who had been seconded from NORWEB to support the Trust's activities in the Kendal area.

My initial involvement with the PYBT brought me into contact with David Kaine, a retired Head of Business Studies at the Furness College of Further Education. David had been involved with the PYBT for several years and he was a cornerstone for the Trust in the Furness area helping to promote the Trust's purpose, and at the same time he was the co-ordinator of the Trust mentors around the Furness area and beyond. David arranged to meet me at my home to explain the methods of working and how he and I would work together to provide networking and help for young people. As well as his accountancy and bookkeeping background he was involved with many social and charity organisations in the area. To this day I consider David as my own guide and mentor. He has unique qualities in being able to express himself clearly and calmly on any subject and forms a strong opinion without been judgemental. His ability to organise and bring people together is exemplary. I envy his skill of shorthand especially when taking minutes of meetings from which he always provided a précis of facts and an accurate representation of what was discussed.

The structure of the PYBT in Cumbria in 1995–2004 was organised so that each applicant could receive the maximum amount of help and support. The support was such that any applicant fitting the PYBT criteria who showed interest or wanted help in setting up in self-employment could receive support in kind or access to funding, through the Trust.

At the time the county head office and staff were supported by BNFL and included manager Alan Hurst, who insisted on good management practices and office procedures and was a powerhouse and a driver of the PYBT in Cumbria. I benefited greatly from being involved with Alan. He was strong willed and principled. He was well supported by Margaret Frost, his deputy, and office staff Christine Vincent-Briggs and Joyce Donaldson. Subsequent managers to Alan Hurst on his retirement in 1996 were Les Hanley, Carl Carter, and Marian Kearney.

In addition there was a volunteer board/panel (see Appendix O) made up of senior people from the county consisting of representatives from industry, banks, accountancies, commerce and public bodies. Their main purpose was to assess the submitted applications against the Trust's criteria and objectives, keeping the interest of the applicant paramount.

On occasions where I had PYBT applicants to represent, I would attend these panel/board meetings and this gave me an insight into how individual board members administered their decision-making process and how they justified their decision.

My involvement with a typical application is outlined in Appendix O, but I was impressed with the PYBT start-up business plan format which was very user friendly and helped the client to think clearly about what was required in the way of business planning. It allowed each part to be broken down into simple small chunks, with useful guidance notes adjacent to the respective parts of the plan. When information was entered in all the respective sections of the plan, no matter how much the detail, it had the makings of a complete and good business plan.

This basic approach was so important to the people we were dealing with and on completion of their application form and business plan I would provide a supplementary report that provided my own perception of relevant information, including their attributes and characteristics for self-employment. This report was sent to the area manager and subsequently formed part of the information that went to the board for them to form a decision. The way the client had approached the initial process of their idea with some evidence of any market research was an indicator of suitability for self-employment.

The conditions for receiving support through the PYBT were that they had to have a realistic and viable chance of some form of development and success in self-employment. Their business idea had to be sound and could be very basic because it wasn't purely considered in terms of profitability but social factors came into play in keeping them in touch with society and it was also important for them not to be taking on something or committing themselves to something that would be unsuitable. Self-employment is a very demanding and a responsible decision even to people who have more support. Our applicants were unable to get support from banks, family or other sources. The Trust was acting as a funder of last resort.

After my initial introduction to the client I would set them small tasks for our next meeting. If they came back with a positive approach and showed initiative I would encourage them to take their ideas further by attending a basic business training course run through Furness Enterprise which covered aspects of marketing, pricing policy, sales, taxation and help in developing their business plan. The evidence of this type of training was mandatory for support from PYBT. The ones who remained negative and didn't push themselves may have needed further motivation and I would encourage them to try and achieve goals no matter how small. If this failed perhaps they were not suited to self-employment and would be more comfortable being employed.

The strong desire to be independent and self-sufficient came through as a positive approach rather than thinking self-employment as an easy option.

To ascertain if the client fitted the PYBT criteria a home visit was arranged by either me or a board member, bearing in mind most were from very deprived areas, but others came from a background where the conventional family and bank support were available. On the other hand, some had a good education but didn't want their parents involved and wanted to go it alone, and a diplomatic approach had to be made not to breach the individual's confidentiality.

My report was sent in and reviewed by the PYBT area manager who might then ask further questions and suggest amendments and adjustments if this would strengthen the case for the applicant. The board would have access to all the paperwork and the report and on most occasions my attendance to answer questions.

The area manager made sure the application was complete and forwarded to a PYBT board/panel for them to decide if approval could be granted and to what level support should be provided. This support could be in the way of grants, loans, test marketing grants and expansion loans, or just mentor guidance (see Appendix O).

Once approved by the board a mentor was allocated to the applicant and prior to the board decisions the area manager and I would have discussed a potential mentor (see Appendix O).

I was involved with the recruitment of mentors and the process had to ensure that the mentor had empathy and would be available when the client had a problem which was not normally just between 9 am to 5 pm. Client problems would occur at all times of day and on weekends when a quick access to a mentor meant the problem was shared and discussed.

Mentor induction programmes were organised in small groups or individually with discussions on the overall duty of a mentor and how they were to operate, giving them enough freedom and flexibility to decide how often and when they met with the client in accordance with the mentoring agreement.

I arranged regular group mentor meetings for the Furness area where they were brought up-to-date with the Trust's activities and how each mentor was progressing with their client. A lot of cross-pollination was provided with different mentors having different degrees of problems and success which other mentors were able to apply.

Of all the clients to which mentors had been allocated I think only twice did I get involved in a mentor–client relationship that wasn't working.

One was with a couple trading in a unit of a craft centre who both had an artistic flair for making handmade craft work and got great satisfaction from producing them. One of the two also taught part-time to supplement their income. The mentor appointed on paper was of suitable experience but he kept insisting they should go into mass production for efficiency, whereas they had not gone into self-employment to do this; they wanted to be hands on. The situation got to a state where communications between them broke down and animosity crept in. I was brought into the situation as an arbitrator and they mutually agreed to break their relationship. This particular mentor went on to mentor more successfully and make good relationships with clients. Part of the problem had been that the mentor was not helping this particular couple with their objectives and was tending to run the business rather than give unconditional help.

The other situation involved a complete breakdown of trust between the mentor and client and this was all over a casual remark by the mentor in a joking mood that dwelled on the client's mind. These small things happen in self-employment and a small problem can niggle and get out of all proportion. Once trust was lost the arrangement had to be terminated.

Sometimes a business didn't require funding and purely required mentoring. Many said that the money was important but the mentoring system was of more value to them. The mentor support could make the difference between success and failure in the early months of starting a business.

The mentor also played an important part in the control of the money forwarded to the client from the Trust. They acted as joint signatories for the money that was deposited with the bank for the items agreed. That way the client could not purchase anything that the money was not allocated for and had been identified in the business plan, although the mentor had flexibility in allowing important expenditure if it arose and wasn't in the business plan.

What I found so useful about the structure of the PYBT in Cumbria was that in about just three phone calls the young disadvantaged person applying through the Trust had access to contacts and support information of the highest level across Cumbria as well as from the PYBT regional and national offices. It was this local network and easy access to support that made a difference and made the mechanism of the Trust work so well in the county.

No matter which area of the county the applicant came from they had senior influential people on hand and I was proud to be part of this assistance and instrumental in helping its operation, especially in the Furness area. None so much as when a young girl came over to me after receiving a County business award and thanked me. I replied, "Any success is all down to you." And she said, "You were the first person I came to for guidance."

The individual board members had their different outlook and reasons why approval should be given or not; the accountants and bankers were interested in figures, the industrialists in the practicality of the business plan; the Bishop and those that felt the applicants should be given a chance took a softer, more social approach. Bill Lowther, the chairman, would summarise the differing opinions and put it to a vote in a well-balanced, constructive and sometimes humorous way, bearing in mind all the time that it was the individual's interest that was paramount.

Often the applicant had been unable to get financial support through the banks in the first place because they were either unemployed or unable to get credit. Once the board approved an application and a mentor was in place banks and other institution would be prepared to lend once they realised the risks were being shared and the support of the PYBT was behind the client.

The types of businesses the PYBT applicants were interested in starting were wide ranging. Some were interested in trading as a business and recruiting staff, but chiefly they were one-person operations, those normally known as "one-man bands" who had a feel for potential customers, a market and a demand for their skill or specialisation. This was typical of those who were interested in providing a service to people and who could set up with very little capital, perhaps working from home but requiring lots of guidance.

Most who enquired were wanting to set up in some service-related business: hairdressing, window cleaning, car valeting and photography, for example. Some were keen on aromatherapy, physiotherapy, singing, fashion design, soft furnishing, and market stalls but some were more forward thinking and had ideas that would create employment for themselves and others. Their business plan normally had to be more comprehensive to assess their viability.

Although the money allocated was to be controlled and spent wisely it was acknowledged that a high percentage would be written off because of the high financial risks that were being taken on. Companies in Cumbria and throughout the country contributed not only in money but a lot in kind to the Trust, by providing the client with office facilities, secretarial support, marketing leaflets and the like, which was extremely useful. One of the offers from the utility companies was that subject to availability they would sell to the client vans which were no longer of use to the company at a very favourable price. This facility helped many to get their businesses off the ground. In many instances I played a role in facilitating this type of support.

When I accepted my role with the PYBT I was also setting up as self-employed myself, and I became aware of all the things that had to be in place prior to starting trading regarding, taxation, National Insurance, expenses, and the use of my home for business, so I was able to pass on some of my own experiences.

I will give three examples of typical applicants I was involved with.

One lad, Douglas Gillam, was only in his teens and interested in drumming and wanted to start a drumming studio where he would teach people to play the drums both for musical and therapeutic reasons.

He developed a business plan and wanted help with a small amount of funding to make use of premises in a habited area. He went to great lengths in obtaining advice from a sound and noise consultant on the specification of his building but after several months of preparing this plan it was eventually turned down by the local council not just because of sound issues but problems of vehicular access.

This didn't put him off. He then developed his business idea by taking on clients in their own premises. He also developed a relationship with the local schools which were interested in developing their musical syllabus to include drumming. This was mainly to do with handicapped children or people who would benefit from the physical and therapeutic benefits of rhythm.

Douglas had the privilege of being introduced to Prince Charles on the occasion when Prince Charles visited the charity Community Action Furness at the Victoria Hall in Rawlinson Street, Barrow-in-Furness in 2003. Not only was he to meet him but he had to "sing for his supper" and provide a drumming session which involved coaching Prince Charles.

Prior to the Prince's arrival at the hall, which had a large open upper level floor space, all the other invited guests, including myself, were asked to form a huge circle around some bins and buckets and Douglas taught the ensemble a few drumming rhythms to be played in unison. When in full swing this was quite a noise. When Douglas was introduced to Prince Charles he demonstrated to him the few beats we had learnt and the Prince became involved. The Prince was a natural and thanked Douglas who mentioned that he had been started up through the PYBT and Prince Charles said in a characteristically twisted mouth reply, "Really?" So from his initial idea and enquiry he had the honour of teaching Prince Charles in his method of tuition.

Another young lad, Guy Newby, who was only nineteen years of age, was made redundant from local hairdressers and having been on a low wage till then had not much to lose by going self-employed. He was rather immature but knew what he wanted and he had some family support which was a big advantage. I talked through his idea with him, and he subsequently produced a business plan, which included the lease of premises, and which was approved by the board and he received a loan and a small grant. During the development of his ideas and plan I had to visit him at his home and at 10.30 am he wasn't up. He came to the door bleary eyed and I thought, this isn't the attribute of a successful businessman. However he managed his hairdressing shop well, hiring the special chairs and equipment, and then he decided he wanted to move premises and expand, and he applied to the Trust for funding. To do this another business plan was required. He was one of the few who after three years of trading was allowed to apply for an expansion loan of up to £3,000. This was approved. Strong support came through his stepfather and the PYBT Business mentor, John Imlach.

I received an enquiry from a girl from Blackburn in Lancashire called Elaine Crook (her mentor was Ian Stephen) who was interested in opening a florist in Arnside which is on the southern coast of Cumbria. The fact she wanted to set up in Arnside meant her application would have to go the the Cumbrian regional office. When I received the enquiry she was attending a business start-up course at Bootstrap Enterprises in Blackburn and her tutor there was keen to get her idea supported. I said to the tutor that part of the process for support was a visit to the applicant and suggested we meet up. I suggested the Tickled Trout Hotel just off the M6 motorway Junction 31a. It would mean a journey for me of about 50 miles and for her of about 10 miles. Her tutor expressed a wish that she would also like to be present when I interviewed Elaine which was no problem as long as it was agreed with her. She also asked if I lived near a railway station and I said yes, Ulverston station is just down the road from me and she said well Bootstrap Enterprises premise are right outside the station in Blackburn.

I agreed to travel by train and meet up with them both at Bootstrap Enterprises. I stayed for over an hour and discussed the criteria for funding and went through her business plan. After the meeting, the tutor said "I am going to review my method of teaching on business start-ups" after she had seen the way I analysed and asked relevant questions about her business plan. I said, "Don't do this because of me; you will have your own standard guidelines." She liked the way I approached all the important factors including those that sometimes get overlooked when you do a business plan for the first time. She would introduce them as part of her lectures.

The application was one that was approved by the board without amendment and not many questions because she had put her case so well and the board had the background information of my visit and assessment.

Elaine started trading and at one stage became a bit uncomfortable about a pending situation. Her property was on lease through an estate agent in Grange and she got word that it might be for sale and she was aware that the shop next door may have been interested in purchasing. Elaine was worried because she couldn't afford to buy. She rang me for advice, not knowing what to do herself. I put her in touch with John Milton of John Milton Fisher in Kendal who ran his own property company and who made himself available free of charge to any PYBT business seeking help, especially on property-related issues. They met up and Elaine's fears were eased. What he told her was that if they sold the property and she was the sitting tenant she was eligible to compensation of up to three times the business rates which at the time were about £4,000 per year, thus making a compensation case of up to £12,000. This would provide money towards relocation if the situation arose. This lifted a huge worry from her mind and was another demonstration of how the Trust supported these young people. One of the problems of self-employment is it can be very lonely having nobody to talk problems over with and small issues can take over, but with the loyal support of a mentor and special advisors these problems can be nipped in the bud.

Part of promoting the businesses set up through the Trust was to allow certain start-up businesses, chiefly craft and service businesses, to attend county shows and national exhibitions. These included the Lowther Horse Trials near Penrith. On one occasion at this event in August 1995 the PYBT team including myself was interviewed by John Holmes of Radio Cumbria on the role of PYBT in Cumbria. Another well-organised and professional event was at the National Exhibition Centre (NEC) at Birmingham. These were heavily subsidised but gave the opportunity for the businesses to market their wares.

At the Lowther Horse trial the PYBT-supported businesses were housed in a separate section of an allocated marquee or latterly combined with the "Made in Cumbria" marquee. This introduced the businesses to promoting their services to the general public and ways of marketing, receiving enquiries and taking orders. It also provided them with a high profile. The Trust also used the Art and Craft Autumn Fair at the NEC and the Gardeners' World Live Exhibition, where nationally selected businesses had areas allocated for their own purpose, usually situated in an annex to the main hall. This was a very high profile venue for these start-up businesses and part of my role and others was to attend these shows to support the young people if they were approached by a potential client and needed some back-up. We were also available to man their stand if they wanted to get a drink or go to the toilet. In the Gardeners' World tent I was asked to cover for a lad who was a landscape gardener and designer while he went to the toilet. He gave me details on how clients could contact him and the brochure he had for any enquiries, but the only thing the public were interested in was a cascading waterfall using a watering cans that was in the corner of the stand more as decoration. At least three people asked me how much it cost and when the lad returned I said they had indicated their interest but I had no idea of its value. He said I should have said £1,000, but I wasn't to know this. It just goes to show you must be prepared for the unexpected.

Another incident occurred when a lad from the Sedbergh/Kendal area was exhibiting his wrought-iron products, including tables and chairs. He had just been approached by a restauranteur for a price for several hundred chairs and tables which he had no experience of quoting for. But with the Trust mentoring and volunteering system we were able to contact a contracts manager in Cumbria who sent him a pro-forma of the tendering document that would fulfil his requirements. This was another example of how when you exhibit you must be prepared for anything and in the end the order was so big he would not have been able to handle it even if he got it.

As part of my duties I was expected to promote the work of the PYBT by giving talks and group discussions to various organisations that may benefit and promote the Trust.

These groups included job centre staff in Barrow, Ulverston, Kendal and Millom who would convey what help the Trust could provide to the young unemployed. Students from Sixth Form colleges, especially ones interested in self-employment, would be told about the PYBT by their senior lecturer who drew it to the attention of students training to be joiners, plumbers, electricians aromotherapists, caterers, beauticians or hairdressers and they would attend one group meeting with me. This was appropriate for any one who was near the end of their training and helped them plan for the future and there was a unit in their NVQ studies which covered business planning.

On one occasion I gave a presentation along with the area manager at the time, Marian Kearney, to the inmates of HM Prison in Haverigg, who were provided with craft courses as part of their rehabilitation. After a group talk I spoke to them individually and when it came to the subject of how to raise finance one lad who wanted to produce garden furniture gave me a knowing look and said "you leave the raising of finance to me"!

I remember giving a presentation to Witherslack Women's Institute and the kind lady who gave the vote of thanks said that she didn't believe such a boring topic could me delivered so well. I think it promoted interest not for them but perhaps for their grandchildren. Not only was I expected to present the talk but as part of the Women's Institute tradition I had to judge the competition of the night which was to do with Royalty Coronation mugs and cups. This was a decision made purely according to my own taste and had nothing to do with antiquity or value!

One of the highlights of my time with the Prince's Trust was to attend a Silver Celebrity Ball in association with Manchester United Football Club at Old Trafford. This was on Thursday, 8th November 2001. We were celebrating the Trust's 25th anniversary since its formation in 1976. This event was attended by stars from television soaps such as *Coronation Street, Holy Oaks, Brookside, Emmerdale,* and international leading sportsman and women including Manchester United players such as Sir Bobby Charlton. An auction took place with Eric Knowles of the *Antiques Roadshow*, selling donated products. This raised a considerable amount of money for the Trust.

Self-employment

To assist in my own self employment activities I converted a bedroom for dual purpose as both bedroom and office, fitted out with desk, cupboards, filing cabinets and a computer. The computer was bought in 1995 from Miller Computer Systems which was a small, local start-up business started by David Miller first in Barrow who then moved to the Lightburn trading estate in Ulverston.

The specification of the computer included: an Intel 2 Pentium 75 Processor with 8 mb RAM expandable to 128 mb, a 1GB EIDE hard drive, supporting software and a printer for a total price of £1,710. This would be considered a lot of money in terms of what can be purchased today.

One of the aspects of being on the consultancy course (CETAD) was having access to the computer room at Lancaster University. Before I got my own computer I used to travel by car to the university, which took about 45 minutes and I would stay for up to four hours processing all my outstanding reports and correspondence. The computer laboratory required card access but you could visit any time, including weekends. On one occasion, when I was fairly recently acquainted with computers, the room was full of students, many of them Chinese, who were busy with their own work. I had typed a piece of work and wanted a copy so I pressed the key for one copy.

However the printer situated towards the rear of the room spouted forth and produced endless copies in heaps of folding, perforated sheets of paper. The machine wouldn't stop and I asked a Chinese student nearby how I could stop it but he just shrugged his shoulders. This was a bit embarrassing. Instead of processing one copy I must have dithered with my finger when typing "1" and entered "111"; I was rewarded with a fair pile of perforated folding paper.

Not only did I make use of the university's computer facilities but I used their library as well. The course taught me the basics of how to use a computer and especially word processing. I'd come from a position where I always had secretarial support at work with all my reports typed by someone else, to starting from scratch using one finger on the keyboard. But I progressed quickly and I can now type as fast as I can talk in slow conversation and keep pace with my thoughts. This was a big factor that changed the way I operated, from using my small, scrawled and sometimes illegible handwriting to a way I could express myself on paper with confidence. It could also be adjusted with ease at anytime and also had the added advantage of "spell check". This application has been a large factor in making writing this book possible.

To keep up-to-date with NDT and quality control matters I attended a National Accreditation of Measurement and Sampling (NAMAS) course at Scarman House, University of Warwick, in December 1995. This course would give me the opportunity to become involved as part of their assessor team. NAMAS is a branch of the United Kingdom Accreditation Service (UKAS) and is responsible for the assessment and accreditation of calibration and testing laboratories. They commission experts to perform assessment on its behalf for a wide range of industries. This would give me a chance to carry out assessments against the NAMAS standard. I was included on a register of potential assessors but never carried out any assessments mainly because the local companies in the area were not involved and the ones in Lancashire were covered by assessors from their area. However the experience kept me up-to-date and the knowledge subsequently provided help to companies I was involved with.

It was on this course I was asked as part of a group discussion the reason for my attending. Part of my reply was that I felt it was part of my apprenticeship for retirement, a way of keeping all my options open which in context isn't a bad policy for people approaching retirement. It makes you aware of the need to think positively and to treat your life as a constant learning experience.

Change of Vision and Perception

After finishing work in 1994 my new freedom and flexibility offered the opportunity to appreciate the finer cycles of time in nature as the trees, flowers and countryside altered. This had never been possible when working from 7.30 am to 5.00 pm. I began to think differently and observe habits and movements which I did not have the time to appreciate when working. I started musing over different things and analysed situations differently. When you work nearly forty years with the same company you certainly get programmed into a set way of thinking and behaving. I would now start to ask myself, when driving say, such things as I wonder where that vehicle is going and what is he carrying? And when I noticed property was being altered, I would consider whether it was to its advantage and cost effective.

How I spent my time could become an issue. On the one hand I didn't want to fritter it away and Doreen was always conscious of me being under her feet and with all this potential time at home it may give me an opportunity for procrastination, but Doreen did not condone this approach and in her judgement there was no shades of grey, just black and white. My nature was normally one of procrastination, researching and then deciding but Doreen never saw it like that and always accused me of "pissing about". She has a far more a practical approach to things than me but my main aim was towards a mixture of outcomes, keeping my mind and body active, leisure time, a mentor to my family and grandchildren and having holidays when it was desired.

It was on Saturday 12th September 1998 that our daughter Susan was married to Ross Anderson a Quantity Surveyor whose family lived in Hartlepool in the North East of England.

Susan met up with Ross when she was in lodgings with a girl called Yvonne in a semi-detached house in Kirkstall Road, Leeds. Yvonne advertised for a further lodger and one of the conditions was that neither of them had to fancy him. Ross was interviewed and selected and as the months went by when Doreen and I would visit Susan, Ross would be in the background always offering to make a cup of tea. When he stood up out of the chair to make a cup of tea and went through the door I noticed how tall he was, the hair on his head just brushed the top of the door jamb. Knowing some useless bits of information I knew that a standard door jamb height was 6 foot, 6 inches. Eventually as time went on, instead of being like an extra in a television soap opera doing menial acting tasks, Ross became a lead player in my daughter's life, and in our lives too, and we welcomed him into the family officially on that day.

The wedding reception was held at The Netherwood Hotel at Grange-over-Sands and just prior to making my speech Yvonne briefly reminded me of the agreement she and Susan had when taking on the additional lodger – that no one had to fancy him – and perhaps she was thinking that I may be short on things to mention. I must say my speech was well accepted and went on for 20 minutes, managing to include Yvonne's statement.

Ross and Susan settled down in Roundhay, a suburb on the north-east side of Leeds, and they have a son, Lewis, the youngest of our grandchildren.

After the PYBT

My role with the PYBT came to an end in March 2004. The structure of the PYBT was altering nationally and rather then being a separate section of the Prince's Trust the business programme became incorporated with the other nine or so programmes of the Prince's Trust and the Cumbria branch was brought more into line with how the other regions operated. Cumbria had operated with some freedom but still within the purpose of the Trust. The area manager became the manager for all the trust programmes in the county.

The outcome of this was that the way I operated was no longer acceptable and I either would have to be employed by the Trust which I was precluded because I was over 60, or be a pure volunteer and carry out my functions on a completely voluntary basis. This was not acceptable to me; the duties I performed involved more time and commitment than would be expected of a volunteer.

I argued my case with representatives of the Trust but they were adamant and, for a charity that was considered entrepreneurial in its promotion of its business programme was rather negative in not accepting my self-employment status. In doing so, they not only lost me and my time, but also the support of Vickers who provided my funding.

The work I did with the Trust from following a person's idea through obtaining funding, appointment of a mentor and networking for people starting self-employment gave me an insight into what was required for business planning.

I still had a base at Furness Enterprise, the local development agency – and what I did with the Trust was complementary to their purpose and mutually beneficial – and I was approached by Val Robinson, the Funding and New Start-Up Manager at Furness Enterprise, and asked if I would consider becoming a business counsellor for them, saying, "If the Trust can't make use of you, *we* certainly can, especially with you having the experience of dealing with young people right through the business start-up process."

This was a natural progression for me and I said I would help out on a need-to-have basis rather than full time or on a contract to do too many hours a week. This suited Val and she could call on me if and when required.

One of the conditions I agreed with Val was to attend a two-day business counselling course in Bolton, Lancashire, organised through the Business Advisors' professional body.

I found this course of value. The lecturer, who was familiar with all the aspects of business counselling prepared the grounding for me. I still refer to the notes that were provided for they were succinctly put and although basically common sense, they brought all the issues together.

The work I had being doing with the PYBT was important because the Trust had procedures in place for dealing with most situations and these became second nature when counselling or guiding people.

To provide some credibility I asked Val if I could be assessed against the counselling standards of the Small Firms Enterprise Development Initiative (SFEDI). I limited this just to pre-start-up businesses because this was my forte rather than advising existing businesses, although I had knowledge of how to do that too.

After agreeing to this I would still have time for my family and grandchildren: David, my son, and Vanessa, my daughter-in-law, have three young children – Dean, Danica and Dane and live in Dalton-in-Furness which is only about four miles away from where I live, and Susan, my daughter, and Ross, my son-in-law, have a young boy called Lewis and they live at Roundhay in Leeds. The grand-children's ages at the time of writing are 17, 16, 11 and six. They have different characteristics, including politeness and charm, but are all quite distinct individuals. Doreen and I have to use our controlling and diplomatic skills to the full, but it is good to see them grow and to spend time with them in a way I was unable to do with my own children while I was working. I enjoy seeing life through their eyes which is a totally different perception from ours; they keep you alive and up to date especially in the field of communication and computers.

Holidays in My Semi-retirement

Doreen and I have made time for holidays, and on average in the earlier years we enjoyed going away once a year but latterly, after 1994, we are managing two a year. The type of holiday we enjoy are the ones which include a package of accommodation and touring and covering selected areas of a country over a period of two to three weeks. We mostly use Titan Hi Tours who have served us well and they were one of the first tour companies to pick you up from home and return you to your home which in our cases meant travelling to Heathrow or Gatwick because Titan don't operate from northern airports but this is never a problem.

Some of the areas we have covered are Alaska, Canada, South Africa, most of the states in North America, Malaysia, Sri Lanka and Finland. We have gone to Madeira with other holiday companies several times including in the Spring, Autumn and over New Year. The only regret we had with Titan was that they did not cover China and we toured China with Saga. I mentioned to Titan that people are interested in visiting China irrespective of human rights, etc., and they were missing out on a potential market. When we returned from China in 2006 a Titan brochure came through the post offering similar tours to China. The holiday in China was the most enjoyable and rewarding of our holidays. It was more than a transitory pleasure for the period we were there but our visit was a holiday that has stayed with us because of all the cultural difference and the potential the country has for business/trade as long as it can combine the state control and the free marketing approach that is developing amongst the new generation of Chinese.

Health Audit and Incidentals

I still maintain my weekly one-hour early morning swim in the local baths and find it enables me to maintain some degree of fitness, suppleness and relaxation and drains away any toxins and stress that may have built up.

It was a surprise for me, having taken up the offer of an over-sixties health check in April 2001, to discover my blood pressure was high (196/102) and it was suggested I lose weight which I did. I lost 22 lbs but although my blood pressure reduced to 165/88, it was not a significant amount. Consequently I had to take blood pressure tablets. This is now monitored and over the years my blood pressure has been normal.

One of the things I do for enjoyment and relaxation is playing my piano, which I changed for a digital one in March 2008. I find this instrument far more versatile than my old freebie piano which I got in the early 1970s which I had to smash up with a crowbar and hammer before taking it to the tip, and the scrapyard gave me £5 for the cast iron frame.

I continued business counselling through Furness Enterprise which includes the programme "Taking the Plunge" which is designed to help people who have a business idea but do not know how to begin. The advantage of this programme after an initial two sessions with a trainer in a classroom situation is the opportunity to take it further with a one-to-one session with a business advisor to talk through their idea and attributes in a non-judgemental manner, covering the aspects of business terminology and business planning. This is desirable for anybody wanting to become self-employed and who is unsure of themselves. This allows them to talk things through and to explore the advantages and disadvantages of self-employment and to ask questions they may feel uncomfortable asking in a classroom or family situation. At the end of each session the person became more aware if, firstly, they had the skills and attributes to run a business, and secondly, if their idea had credibility and viability. Conversely it gave them the option after our discussion to realise that self-employment may not be for them.

At one of the business network meetings I attended at the Netherwood Hotel at Grange-over-Sands, Tony Eva gave a presentation on how he started his business, Teva Ltd, a small family firm in Dalton-in-Furness, which provides a Preventative, Maintenance and Condition Monitoring service.

During his presentation I felt I should know him because the type of work and the training requirements of staff were similar to the ones I had been used to in my working life and his type of work was like a sister application and complimentary to non-destructive testing. Teva help to solve problems caused by vibrations and over-heating of moving and rotating parts in mechanical and electrical machinery.

Although I was attending the meeting with my business hat on I went over to him and explained that with my engineering, NDT, and inspection background I may be able to provide some support, and I asked if he would mind if I visited him. He made me very welcome and realised he could use my knowledge and experience. Over the years I have built up a good relationship with the family – his son Ian and daughter Louise – and their secretary Eileen who brings her strong secretarial and administration skills to the company, as well as the engineers they employ, and have acted as a type of non-executive director, able to see things from outside the vagaries of small businesses.

I maintain an interest in photography and attend the Ulverston Photographic Club meetings, struggling to keep up with all the advances in digital photography. I find it unnatural to be able to take an image and alter it substantially after the event. It makes me feel a rogue rather than a technical person producing images that are factual and authentic. Some pictorial images produced can be pure fiction. At one time photographs could be used as supporting evidence in arguments and disputes. So much can now be altered and the image can bear no relationship to the original and may misrepresent the situation.

Doreen and I still live in the bungalow we bought in 1966, with a few additions and modifications but it is a home where we have raised our children which they still make a base with the grandchildren. The modifications are modest but have been carried out by people I admire for different reasons, including Tony Anderson director of House of Anderson's from Morecambe who provided us with a conservatory in 1999, and Mike Hughes Kitchens/Bedrooms who have done alterations inside the house. I admire Andersons for their practical and personal touch, and Mike Hughes for his preciseness, attention to detail and professionalism. Both these two companies were not the lowest quotations but their approach and customer satisfaction have given us piece of mind.

Doreen also enhanced the property not only by her presence but with her household skills, including, decorating, painting, wall papering, gardening and, none the least, here excellent cooking skills and table preparation. The grandchildren aren't impressed by her discipline but love her food. Her input to the domestic policy and its implementation is way above my contribution. Her forthrightness, in a way which I could not have portrayed, has been my backbone. I was more for controlling and budgeting than using energy and creative skills.

Doreen's passion for etiquette and strong principles prompts our daughter to sometimes say, "Mother, you may have to lower your standards", but this is so ingrained like "Blackpool" is through Blackpool rock and the only way you would get rid of it is by eating her, although she is starting to mellow with age.

We have been privileged in having good neighbours, especially Mildred Davis who was widowed and came from Foxfield near Broughton in-Furness to be our immediate neighbour in September

1975. She died in September 2010, but she maintained her sense of humour to the end and was a proud and principled lady who was spot-on and up-to-date with local and family information.

CHAPTER SEVEN

2004–
Three Score Years and Ten, Plus
Reflections

"Was I tight or just careful?"

Perhaps the time has arrived for reflection; I still have a positive mind and outlook, always wanting to stay one step ahead of the average of my peer group. Again you might say it is an apprenticeship for the inevitable although attitude, aspiration and perception with a time for reflection are the ingredients for staying connected to society.

How wise would it be to capitalise on all my existing knowledge, rather than expend energy trying to obtain more knowledge with diminishing returns! But there is a certain amount of comfort and satisfaction from keeping up to date.

I don't think you can underestimate the value of responsibility being given or thrust upon you at an early age. Some students today can proceed through school, college and University up to the age of 24 without having any real responsibility on their shoulders other than attending tuition classes, and passing examinations. It then becomes difficult for them to fit into the world of work and later family responsibility if they have always been cushioned from the realities of life. By all means obtain an education but this should include elements of real life situations. Many who try and achieve a high academic qualification suffer later because they cannot easily apply the information in the real world. Some graduates may be no more than an encyclopaedia on a library shelf. An optimum would combine education, experiences and having the mentoring support of a person to look up to as role model and provide an example on how you may like to conduct your affairs.

My approach to life has been one where I have been able to quantify, measure or relate to some benchmarking. This approach gives a life of calculations and outcomes but does not bring into consideration how you evaluate emotions, feelings, satisfaction and contentment. I always remember a scientific quote that stated that if you cannot express yourself in numbers your knowledge is of a meagre nature and you have not yet achieved the art of science, and this, in my mind, could include any subject you were expressing opinions on. People who say "Oh, it's not far," or "They have a lot of money," or "My car is good on petrol," or "He is on a good wage," may be generalising but do not give the impression that they really know what they are talking about. Because it is all relative.

I am at ease when I am dealing with a precise question and applying my knowledge rather than a vague question that needs creative answers.

I now appreciate the importance of individual/group creative flair in establishing enterprise, long before the hard facts and figures come into the equation, including accountants, marketing specialists, employment and the taxman.

I may not have made a fortune for myself or other organisations, but on the other hand I haven't lost one.

Over a lifetime I will have spent as much money as anybody else in my peer group and no one in their wildest dreams would say I have been reckless with my money or anybody else's.

Happiness and success is difficult to define and accomplish but contentment at whatever level is rewarding and comforting.

I have often explained how important music can be in people's lives, the way it relaxes you and reduces stress, especially if you play musical instruments where you fingers are in contact with the vibration of strings or a vibrating medium. It is an analogy to stress relieving processes in steel manufacture and metal work whereby great stresses are introduced in the way the metal is handled and formed. There develops a need to relieve those stresses. This is done by heating to above a critical temperature and then lowering gradually until the built-in stresses are relived. This is what music is capable of.

The whole process of life and creation revolves around vibrations, pulsing, spinning, rotating, changing energy levels and the body is no different.

There is a large contrast to the way I saw my parents to how my own children and especially the grandchildren perceive me. I suppose like my parents did, and we have all adapted to the environment of our time. When you think of how easy the grandchildren are coping with the communication technology. All have access to computers and mobile phones. I suppose you have to give them their heads because they will probably cope better with the things to come than we will and we only hope it gives rise to a satisfying and fulfilling life with a hope of a stable family life.

I regularly provide after-school grandchildren duty when their parents are at work. While as a working man I never had the opportunity to spend that sort of time with my own children, as Doreen keeps telling me. She would often say "You only knew one half of what went on in this household", but I remind her flippantly that I knew about the *important* half.

What were just ancillary activities to going to work, such as collecting a newspaper or going for a hair cut, now becomes a project on its own and activities such as seeing doctors, opticians, and dentists, as well as attending funerals put a constraint on the time available to do other things and if you're not careful can become the core business of your life in retirement.

What value do you place on being married to Doreen for nearly 50 years plus the 6 years of courtship, plus two children and 4 grandchildren who all put your life into perspective and how their own individual characteristics and attributes have enriched your life and the environment you were brought up in.

Doreen is always saying to me there are no pockets in a shroud and I again flippantly tell her that I have it on good authority there is a good exchange rate up there.

But I would say I have always had a responsible approach and any decisions I have made have been well balanced, and rarely extended beyond my comfort zone.

Apart from all the people and circumstances that have influenced me, I should also acknowledge Messers Luck (good and bad), Opportunity and Timing. Most people who have been successful have had an element of some or all these people.

I consider myself a competent technician, supervisor, manager and a respected parent but only my children will be able to objectively judge the latter. I have tried to lead by example not in a dictatorial way, letting them exercise their own feelings and intentions and only stepping in if I considered a situation serious enough to warrant it, by offering suggestions and guidance. Imposing your views and opinions on the next generation may intimidate them and not allow them to take their own path. They have to learn by their own mistakes and own judgement.

I have probably imposed limitations on my self rather than wait for society to do so. I have been aware of being promoted to a level of incompetence as per the "Peter Principle" where eventually you are raised to a level of incompetence.

Without reaching your limit your potential is unlimited but once the limit, peak or zenith is reached there is only one way to go.

Even as an 11-plus failure opportunities arose to develop my skills and interest and which gave me a feeling of worth and satisfaction. Perhaps that may have not been so if I had gone down an academic career I was not suited to!

I have survived through discipline and commitment rather than raw talent and I feel content and at ease of how I have conducted my affairs and I hope I have provided responsible guidance not only to my family but others who seek it. But still I don't understand why I am here, other than some big master plan that is in progress which I'm not fully aware of.

I wrote this book to portray who I am, what I did and the people and events that influenced me on my journey. These factors drew me to higher levels of thinking and application that formed part of my subconscious and was not based on qualifications alone. This underlying theme makes you different and forms your character. I hope who I am is self explanatory and in addition I would like to recall some of those people I have mentioned.

My Mother	for her gentleness and tenderness
My Father	for his lack of fear and pain
My sister Enid	for her strength of character to fight and

	accept an inherent bronchial condition
My wife Doreen	for her love, consideration and pride in family and her work ethic
Old Bob, father-in-law	for his values in life and lack of interest in material wealth
Brian Lennon	for leadership qualities
Brian Wood	for his business and marketing skills
Harry Rea	for his supervisory attributes
Ron Slater	for his management and business lecturing skills, knowledge and modesty
David Kaine	for his mentoring and guidance skills
Wilf Cotton	for working things out from basic principles

All the above are of a similar age to me or older and some are no longer with us. Having been involved with senior people to me I was able to learn from their knowledge and experience, but I also admire many younger people in the way they conduct themselves and their lives. I may not have the opportunity for them to profoundly affect my future which may fall back on my immediate family when I may have to seek guidance on my journey to the finishing line.

A Poem to Finalise My Thoughts

The life I've lead may not have been exciting
Although it has been most fulfilling and rewarding
Inspired by the application of contentment and containment
Never built up on speculation and dreaming
Always having the feeling of gradually moving forward
Not in severe stop, go, or reverse situation
Never wanting to loose the ground already made
But build upon it and consolidate
In hoping that my family
Have benefited from my approach
Of leading by example
Rather than providing a crutch for support.

Glossary of Terms & Acronyms

ASNT	American Society of Non-destructive Testing
B&B	Bed and Breakfast accommodation
BNFL	British Nuclear Fuels Limited
CETAD	Centre for Continuing Education Training and Development
CT	Computerised Tomography
GCE	General Certificate of Education "O" & "A" Level
KONVER	EU support programme which encourages the arms industry to convert to civilian activities
milisieverts	Measure of effective whole-body dose of radiation
NAMAS	National Accreditation of Measurement and Sampling
NDT	Non-destructive Testing
NORWEB	North West Electricity Board
NVQs	National Vocational Qualifications
PT	Prince's Trust
PYBT	Prince's Youth Business Trust
SFEDI	Small Firms Enterprise Development Initiative
UKAS	United Kingdom Accreditation Service
VICKERS	(Broad name to include Vickers Shipbuilding and Engineering Ltd (VSEL), BAE Systems Submarine Solutions, GEC takeovers when applicable

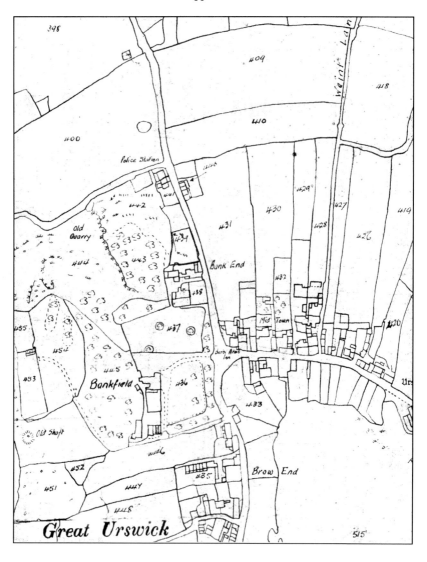

Appendix A Map of Bank End c. 1933

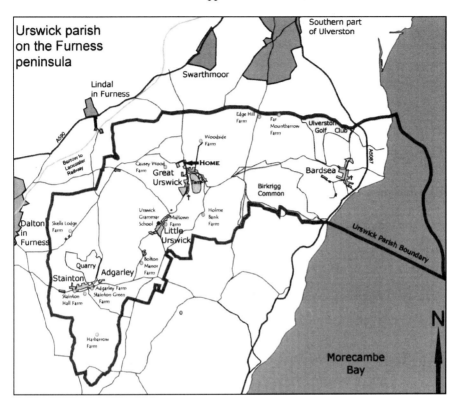

Appendix B Map of Urswick Parish

URSWICK GRAMMAR SCHOOL

REPORT   Summer   TERM 1948

NAME Geoffrey Elleray   CLASS I STANDARD IIIB

SUBJECT	TOTAL POSSIBLE	MARKS GAINED	CLASS POSITION	REMARKS
READING	20	16	2	Good.
SILENT READING	20	7	8	Must improve. Does not concentrate
RECITATION	20	9	9	Not good enough.
COMPOSITION	50	24	3	Very fair.
DICTATION	20	19	1	Very good.
ARITHMETIC.	50	30	1	Capable but careless.
WRITING	20	17	2	Very good.
DRAWING	40	28	5	Good on the whole.
NATURE STUDY	40	12½	8	Not keen enough.
GENERAL KNOWLEDGE.	20	6	8	Poor. Poor listener to wireless.
	300	168½	5/9	

CONDUCT.	Good.
ATTENDANCE.	Satisfactory.
PROGRESS.	Is too easily satisfied. Harder work required.

M. H. Dobson.

- E Elleray. 15/7/48

Appendix C(1) School Report 1948

178

URSWICK GRAMMAR SCHOOL REPORT.
SUMMER TERM 1950.

NAME Geoffrey Elleray   CLASS I   STANDARD IV A.

SUBJECT	Total possible	Marks gained	Class position.	REMARKS.
READING	20	15	4	Good.
SILENT READING	80	63	3	Good.
RECITATION.	20	11	7	Very fair.
COMPOSITION	50	34	2	Good. Classwork not so good.
DICTATION	20	18	6	Very good.
ARITHMETIC	70	69	1	Excellent.
WRITING	20	13	8	Could improve it.
PAINTING	40	32	8	Good.
NATURE STUDY	40	18½	10	Good, but not concerning flowers.
GENERAL KNOWLEDGE	40	27	5	A good listener to wireless programmes. Is interested in the world around him.
	400	300½	4/13	

CONDUCT   Quite satisfactory.

ATTENDANCE   Good. A pity he has odd absences on health grounds.

PROGRESS   Good.

M. H. Dobson.

E Elleray

1949

Nature Record

Snow.	Hail	Frost.	Mist.	Rain.	Dull
⌇ ⌇ ⌇	o o o o				
Very Dull	Rain-bow	Sun	Sun and cloud	Wind	Thunder and Lightning

Appendix D(1) My School Nature Record 1949

Jan '49

Sun rises 8.2 am   Sun sets 4.09 pm

	Sun	Mon	Tues	Wed	Thur	Fri	Sat
WEATHER							
WIND	IV.	W	W	N W	W.	W.	S. W
TEMP Max/Min		Max 52 Min —	Max 43° Min 41°	Max 50 Min 40½°	Max 54° min 33	Max 5½° Min 40	Max Min
RAIN	·02"	·06"	·06"	·02"	·10"	·19"	·43"

9/1/49. Primrose, Aconite, yellow Avens, Celandine
Mouse with slug in its mouth

10/1/49 Ladybird

11/1/49 Barn owl seen 9 A.M

14/1/49 Partridge seen near Church. Mr. Woods's
horse fell with load grain broke and a shaft.

15/1/49 Mr. Soosey's cow ill with a chill.
Holmbank has had 4 calves died since
Xmas

hrs of daylight 8hrs7 mins.47   hrs of darkness 15hrs16 mins½

Appendix D(2) My School Nature Record 1949

Appendix E Ration Book

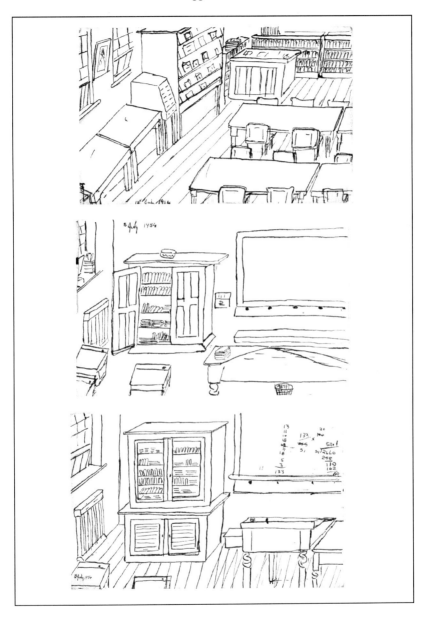

Appendix F1 My Secondary School Sketches: library, form room and maths room

Appendix F2 My Secondary School Sketches: view from bedroom window, the house, and Harry Stable's lorry

WINTER

The winter winds are blowing,
They howl between the trees.
Snow will soon be falling,
And the ponds begin to freeze.

The snow comes falling faster down,
And everything is quiet,
The fields are turned from green and brown
To a smooth sparkling white.

The birds, they have migrated
Into distant warmer lands,
They always fly together
In broad continuous bands.

Soon the winter is ended
And birds begin to sing,
It seems as if their voices blend
Into a merry ring.

GEOFFREY ELLERY
(Form 3A)

THIRLMERE HOUSE NOTES.

Thirlmere had its 'ups and downs' in the
Season 1953 - 1954. The Senior Football Team with
a bit more luck could have finished higher in the
table, as they only lost to Grasmere by one goal to
nil and to Coniston by three goals to two. We
managed to conquer Rydal by three goals to one. The
Junior team won one game out of the three by beating
Rydal one goal to nil. In the final position
Thirlmere came third.

The cricket team did not do so well, not winning
a match, but losing to Rydal by only four runs in an
exciting game.

In the Athletics, Thirlmere became second in
the sports and third in the cross-country, even
though there was keen competition by every house in
both events.

The Senior Girls did better in the Netball
Matches by beating Coniston, drawing with Rydal but
unfortunately losing to Grasmere while the Junior
Girls had excellent results winning all three matches
and gaining six points for the House. These good
results, however, were not kept up in the Rounders
Games and the girls won only one against Rydal by
four to one.

Well, hard Luck Thirlmere, see if next season
can bring more effort from everyone to get better
results in every event.

G. ELLERY. (Capt.)

Appendix G School Magazine Poem and House Captain's Report

Vickers-Armstrongs (Engineers)
Limited

Naval Construction Works

Barrow~in~Furness

Certificate of Apprenticeship

This is to Certify

that Mr Geoffrey Elleray

was employed by us as an Apprentice

Metallurgist

from 17th October 1955. to 15th October 1960.

at which date he satisfactorily completed

his Apprenticeship.

Signed for Vickers-Armstrongs (Engineers) Limited.

C.A.L.Dunphie

(MAJ.-GEN. SIR CHARLES DUNPHIE, C.B., C.B.E., D.S.O.)
CHAIRMAN

GENERAL MANAGER.

DATE 31st January 1961.

Appendix H Certificate of Apprenticeship

VICKERS-ARMSTRONGS (ENGINEERS) LIMITED.

AGREEMENT OF APPRENTICESHIP.

This Agreement made the _17th_ day of _July,_ One thousand nine hundred and _Fifty Six,_ between _Geoffrey Ellray,_ (hereinafter called " the Apprentice ") a minor of _16_ years of age on the _13th_ day of _December,_ One thousand nine hundred and _Fifty Four,_ of _1, Bank End Terrace, Great Urswick, Ulverston,_ and _Ernest Ellray,_ (hereinafter called " the Guardian ") of _1, Bank End Terrace, Great Urswick, Ulverston,_ and _Vickers-Armstrongs (Engineers) Limited,_ (hereinafter called " the Company ") of _Barrow-in-Furness._

WITNESSETH that with the consent of the Guardian testified by the latter's execution of this Agreement the Apprentice has agreed to serve the Company, and the Company has agreed to accept and pay for such service upon the conditions hereinafter contained.

1. The Apprentice and the Guardian jointly and severally agree with the Company as follows :—

   (1) The Apprentice will as from the _17th_ day of _October,_ One thousand nine hundred and _Fifty Five,_ serve the Company for a total period of _Five,_ years of service, each year to consist of fifty-two working weeks calculated in accordance with the provisions of this Agreement, which total period is hereinafter called " the period of service."

   (2) The Apprentice will during the period of service—
      (a) observe and be subject to the conditions of employment contained in the schedule annexed hereto ;
      (b) obey the lawful orders of the Company or their representatives ;
      (c) promote to the best of his ability the interests of the Company.

   (3) The Apprentice will not during the period of service—
      (a) reveal the secrets of the Company's business ;
      (b) do or suffer to be done any damage or other injury to the property of the Company or their customers ;
      (c) absent himself, except in the event of sickness, from the service of the Company without their permission or consent ;
      (d) take part in any labour dispute which may arise between the Company and any of their employees or in which the Company and any of their employees may be involved, nor during the continuance thereof refuse to do any work which the Company may lawfully require him to perform.

2. In consideration of the said obligations undertaken by the Apprentice and the Guardian, the Company agrees with the Apprentice and the Guardian that, subject to the provisions of this Agreement, they will for and during the period of service—

   (1) receive the Apprentice into their service and, subject to the fulfilment by the Apprentice of the said obligations, allow the Apprentice to continue therein until the expiration of the period of service ;

Appendix I(1) Apprenticeship agreement

(2) observe the conditions of employment and pay to the Apprentice in respect of his service wages at the rates contained in the schedule annexed hereto ;

(3) permit the Apprentice to enjoy the advantage of acquiring under the control of the Company to such extent as is practicable, having regard to the conditions of work and of organisation from time to time existing in the Works or in the particular department thereof in which the apprentice may be working, a practical knowledge of the trade of.....*metallurgist*.... so far as from time to time that trade is being carried on in the Works or in such department and the capacity and proficiency of the Apprentice admits.

3. It is further expressly agreed by and between the Apprentice and the Guardian and the Company as follows :—

(1) If the Apprentice shall wilfully disobey the lawful orders of the Company or their representatives or shall persistently neglect or refuse to comply with the provisions of this Agreement or shall grossly misconduct himself or shall habitually absent himself from work without the Company's permission or consent, except in the event of sickness certified by a duly qualified medical practitioner, the Company may without notice suspend the Apprentice for a period without wages or discharge the Apprentice from their service, in which latter event this Agreement will forthwith be at an end.

(2) If by reason of being unable to obtain materials or in consequence of any accident or trade dispute or trade depression or of any cause beyond their control, the Company find it necessary from time to time to close down the Works or any particular department thereof in which the Apprentice may at the time being be working, or to reduce the volume or alter the character of the work done in such Works or such particular department thereof so that the Apprentice cannot continue to be usefully employed or enjoy the facilities for acquiring a practical knowledge of the said trade, the Apprentice will not be entitled to claim to work, or enjoy such facilities, during such time as the Works or such particular department is closed down, nor to claim during such period of reduction or volume or alteration of character of work, to work or to enjoy such facilities save on such basis of short time as the Company may think it best to adopt ; and during such period of closing down or short time the provisions of this Agreement with the exception of Clause 1 (3) (a) will cease to apply either to the Apprentice and the Guardian or to the Company in respect of any working time which the Apprentice by reason of such closing down or short time is not working. Provided that if in any one year of service the Apprentice be prevented under the operation of this clause from working for a total period exceeding four weeks or be required to work on short time during more than twelve weeks, the Apprentice and the Guardian may by notice in writing signed by both of them and addressed to the Company determine this Agreement.

(3) In the event of the apprenticeship being interrupted by the Apprentice undergoing compulsory national service the provisions of this Agreement with the exception of Clause 1 (3) (a) shall during his absence thereon cease to apply either to the Apprentice and the Guardian or to the Company. On the completion of the period of compulsory national service the Apprentice shall within a period of 28 days resume the apprenticeship with a view to its completion on the same terms and conditions subject to any modification necessary in his case in accordance with the requirements of any Interrupted Apprenticeship Arrangements or reinstatement conditions included in the National Service Acts which may be applicable to him.

4. All apprentices will be employed in the first place on probation for a period of six months. The existing regulations and normal scale of pay for apprentices will apply during this probationary period.

Signed by the Apprentice and the Guardian, and by or on behalf of the Company as follows :—

Geoffrey Elleray ....Apprentice.

Wm M Topham ....Witness.

E Elleray ....Guardian.

Rw Gillespie ....Witness.

W. O. G... .

For and on behalf of Vickers-Armstrongs (Engineers) Limited.

...........................Witness.

IMPORTANT. It is important that the Company be notified of any change of address.

Appendix I(2) Apprenticeship agreement

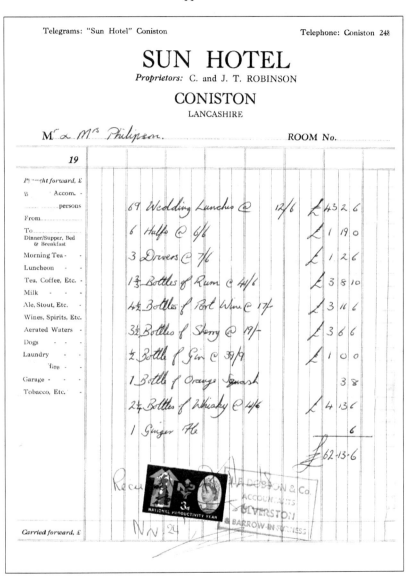

Telegrams: "Sun Hotel" Coniston   Telephone: Coniston 248

SUN HOTEL
Proprietors: C. and J. T. ROBINSON

CONISTON
LANCASHIRE

Mr & Mrs Philipson.   ROOM No.

19			
Brought forward, £			
B Accom. -			
.........persons	69 Wedding Lunches @ 12/6	£43 2 6	
From..........			
To.........	6 Halfs @ 6/6	£1 19 0	
Dinner/Supper, Bed & Breakfast			
Morning Tea -	3 Dinners @ 7/6	£1 2 6	
Luncheon -			
Tea, Coffee, Etc. -	1½ Bottles of Rum @ 41/6	£3 8 10	
Milk - - -			
Ale, Stout, Etc. -	4½ Bottles of Port Wine @ 17/-	£3 16 6	
Wines, Spirits, Etc.			
Aerated Waters -	3½ Bottles of Sherry @ 19/-	£3 6 6	
Dogs - -			
Laundry - -	½ Bottle of Gin @ 39/9	£1 0 0	
Hire -			
Garage - - -	1 Bottle of Orange Squash	3 8	
Tobacco, Etc.			
	2½ Bottles of Whisky @ 41/6	£4 13 6	
	1 Ginger Ale	6	
		£62 13 6	
Carried forward, £			

Appendix J Wedding Receipt

This picture shows the " Ossick Coot," owned and raced by the Urswick Sea S c o u t s, which took part in the " Soap Box Derby " at Scarborough in 1951. The boys are left to right:—J. Mossop, R. Wilkinson, M. Oldcorn and G. Elleray.

'OSSICK COOT' IN SOAP BOX DERBY FINALS

THE soap box track pedal car "Ossick Coot," owned and raced by Urswick Sea Scouts, won its way to the National finals of the "Soap Box Derby" at the semi-finals held at Salford on Saturday.

Driven by 17-years-old Maurice Oldcorn, it won its heat easily in the senior scout group, but was beaten in the second heat. By virtue of its first heat victory, however, ' Ossick Coot " will be seen in the finals at Scarborough in September.

In the ordinary scout group, the car could only gain fourth place in the first heat, the 1st Whitehaven Troop's "Dazzle" coming third. In this race the Urswick driver was 13-years-old Geoffrey Elleray.

The races were held on the pattern of the real thing. Cars were parked and overhauled in the pits between heats in which they ran in groups of five or six. Many spectacular spills were greatly enjoyed by the crowd at the Littletown Road track.

"Ossick Coots" mechanics were Raymond Wilkinson and James Mossop, the party was in the charge of A. S. M. Irving Gawling. There were nearly 50 competitors.

Appendix K Soapbox Derby, Press Cuttings

190

BY APPOINTMENT TO HIS ROYAL HIGHNESS: Business trust certificate winners and dignitaries (back, from left) Tom Dutson, David Hitchen, Steven Denison, Darren Webster, Mark Lamb and Cumbria trust chairman Bill Lowther. Front (from left) trust co-ordinator Geoff Elleray, Furness MP John Hutton, Cheryl Thomas, William Todd, Sara Abbotson, Gillian Fairclough, Vanessa Goude and trust chief executive Richard Street RONNIE KERSHAW Ref: 95171

Appendix L Princes Trust Press Cutting

'Mr NDT' became an X-ray expert

X-ray founder Geoff Elleray.

THE LAST founder member of VSEL's X-ray department has left the Barrow shipyard.

Geoff Elleray, 55, was one of five people who set up the X-ray facility during the late 1950s, in the early days of the nuclear submarine programme.

The department developed into an extensive Non-Destructive Testing (NDT) organisation with Geoff — sometimes known as 'Mr NDT' — one of its leading exponents. "They were the pioneering days," he said.

Geoff took voluntary redundancy, from his post as quality control manager non-destructive engineering, after more than 38 years at VSEL.

Variety

He started work as an apprentice metallurgist in 1955. He became an NDT technician in 1960, a supervisor in 1964, senior radiographer in 1972, and joined NDT management in 1978.

"I enjoyed it all... the variety of work and the problems," he said.

He helped install the HMS *Vulcan* steam-raising plant at Dounreay in the early 1960s, and returned to carry out refits in 1967 and 1972.

He hopes to continue using his NDT expertise by providing help and advice to other companies on a part-time basis.

Geoff plays several musical instruments, including the piano and penny whistle.

Lifetime award for ex-Vickers man

A FURNESS expert at testing materials has been given a prestigious lifetime achievement award.

Geoffrey Elleray received the award from the North Atlantic section of the American Society of Non Destructive Testing at the society's annual conference in Bristol.

It recognises a considerable contribution and achievements in the field of non destructive testing.

Mr Elleray, who lives in Ulverston is, well known in the non destructive testing arena, having started as an apprentice metallurgist which included non destructive testing, in Vickers Armstrong's shipyard laboratory in 1955.

He was involved in aspects of NDT, inspection and quality, covering the nuclear submarine projects as well as commercial engineering and armament contracts.

He left in 1994 as NDT and inspection manager in the quality control department, and set up his own NDT and quality assurance consultancy.

Mr Elleray is also known for providing business start up counselling and advice service for the local enterprise agency Furness Enterprise, and the Prince's Trust.

LONG SERVICE: Geoffrey Elleray, who was given a lifetime achievement award

Appendix M Press cuttings. Top: VSEL Link Magazine, issue 97, May 1994
Bottom: NW Evening Mail, 15th May 2006

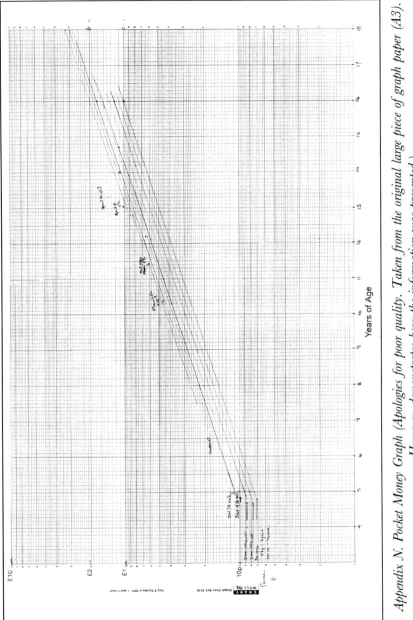

Appendix. N. Pocket Money Graph (Apologies for poor quality. Taken from the original large piece of graph paper (A3). However, demonstrates how the information was presented.)

Appendix O
Notes on The Prince's Youth Business Trust

The Prince's Youth Business Trust (PYBT) operates nationally on a regional and county basis including Cumbria. The Trust was set up by Prince Charles to provide support to young people aged between age 18 and 30 who fit into categories such as unemployed, educational underachievers, ex-offenders or disadvantaged in some way to help them build their self confidence and self esteem and if they had ideas for starting up in business they would be encouraged to develop their idea and take it further. Some of the youngster applying would be interested in working for themselves and they must be made aware of the advantages and disadvantages, some had ideas and personality to form businesses that eventually would take on staff. The support was in the way of grants and cheap loans. The scheme also involved the use of mentors to guide and support the young person in their early stage of starting self employment.

Members of The Cumbria Board

The Board members at the time included; Bill Lowther Chairman, Robin Burgess, Brigader Howard, Ray Davies, Peter Redshaw, Susan Thornly, Terry James, George Coulthard, Graham Foster, Ken Dixon, Arthur Sanderson, Grahame Smith, Hilary Scott, Bill Swarbrick and the Bishop of Penrith, they covered the large county of Cumbria which is divided by the Lakeland mountains and fells and includes the area north of Carlisle and down to the southern tip such as Milnthorpe and Ravonstonedale. With this representation of board members wherever the board meeting was arranged there was always enough board members present to carry out their duties and a quorum for decision making. Over a period of time board members left and new ones were taken on.

Route of a typical application

The initial request would come from the individual to the area head office at Moor Row in West Cumbria and the ones for Furness area were forwarded to me. It was my duty to initially contact the person to empathise and see how the Trust may help. This was done either by telephone or them coming to see me at Furness Enterprise. I would talk them through their idea and see if they complied with **PYBT** criteria for support. This could lead into further information being required from the applicant and the chance to attend further business training to be able to develop their idea and business plan as well as gain and understand the basic principles for starting self employment.

Support Provided

The board apportioned the amount of grant/ loan requested. As a matter of interest at the time the subsidised loans were up to £5000, Grants up to £1500 and Test marketing Grant of up to £250 if the board had decided the applicant had not provided sufficient evidence of a market for the applicants business and this would allow them to test the market by attending trade fairs, marketing and publicity material and after three years of trading they could apply for a £3,000 expansion loan.

Mentor

A mentor is a volunteer who was aware of the Trusts objectives and offered their services to the Trust. Normally these were people with experience of business or association with business and were prepared to help in a friendly, objective manner. The client should not feel intimidated or pressurised. The mentor would not run the business for them but look at it from an overseer's point of view which would help to provide self confidence, motivation and help in overcoming difficult circumstances as well as discussing problems, pitfalls and opportunities. And importantly be contactable when the client needs guidance. The allocation of mentor, which was normally for a period of up to three years, had to take into consideration personalities and any conflict of interest that may arise which could cause embarrassment or be detrimental to the relationship. Many relationships continued after this period, on a friendly basis. In the end after all the support obtained through **PYBT** the problems and solution remained with the individual.

Index
of Names

Index of Names

Index of Names

Index

of Subjects